Editors
Casey Null
Gisela Lee

Editorial Manager
Karen J. Goldfluss, M.S. Ed.

Editor in Chief
Sharon Coan, M.S. Ed.

Illustrator
Ana Castanares

Cover Artist
Jeff Sutherland

Art Coordinator
Denice Adorno

Creative Director
Elayne Roberts

Imaging
Ralph Olmedo, Jr.

Product Manager
Phil Garcia

Trademarks
Trademarked names and graphics appear throughout this book. Instead of listing every firm and entity which owns the trademarks or inserting a trademark symbol with each mention of a trademarked name, the publishers aver that they are using the names and graphics only for editorial purposes and to the benefit of the trademarked owner with no intention of infringing upon that trademark.

Publishers
Rachelle Cracchiolo, M.S. Ed.
Mary Dupuy Smith, M.S. Ed.

Learning Centers
for
Intermediate Classrooms

Written and Compiled by

Casey Null and Patti Sima, M.A.

Teacher Created Materials, Inc.
6421 Industry Way
Westminster, CA 92683
www.teachercreated.com

©2000 Teacher Created Materials, Inc.
Reprinted, 2000
Made in U.S.A.

ISBN-1-57690-508-X

Table of Contents

Table of Contents

Table of Contents

Introduction

Learning centers are a wonderful way to encourage independent learning, add creative reinforcement to more structured lessons, and allow students to work at a comfortable pace. Learning centers may be an integral part of a unit of study or a reward for having completed the day's assignments. Learning centers make it possible for teachers to be in more than one place at a time. Teachers are able to work with groups of students while sending individual students or pairs to learning centers. This book will supplement your good ideas with a potpourri of additional ideas which can be placed in the various learning centers.

What Is a Learning Center?

A learning center is an area in a classroom where one or more children can participate in activities designed for enrichment and review of current learning and for reinforcement of the skills being taught. A learning center coordinated with the curriculum enhances skills and learning.

A center can consist of games, activities, manipulatives, or reading materials. A listening center with special equipment such as a tape recorder with headphones, a computer, calculator, or typewriter may constitute a center. As new topics are introduced or areas of special interest develop, new centers may be created. Rather than serve as primary instruction, a learning center supports what is taught in the classroom. A center provides an alternative to the traditional concept of seatwork. It allows the student an opportunity to independently practice skills and assume responsibility for learning, while freeing the teacher to work with small groups or individual students.

Why Should I Use a Learning Center?

Children learn best when they are actively involved in learning. Manipulating math materials, writing and publishing their own stories, creating plays, exploring the world through maps and globes, or reviewing new vocabulary words are just a few of the learning center activities that provide students with hands-on involvement. Centers accommodate different learning styles which, in turn, give students an opportunity to become more creatively involved in their own education.

Learning centers also help students learn how to work independently. As students want to find the answers for themselves, they become more responsible for completing tasks, checking them, and cleaning up. As patterns for using the centers are established, organizational skills develop.

The nature of the learning center gives students freedom to learn on their own. They begin to think more critically and solve problems. Specific activities may require higher levels of thinking, as well as providing an environment that is conducive to this kind of learning.

Learning Centers for Intermediate Classrooms provides a sampling of a variety of learning center activities that are ready to use with little or no preparation. The activities will supplement classroom studies in the areas of Language Arts, Math, Science, Social Studies, Technology, and for a fun way to reinforce all subjects, Games and Puzzles.

How Do I Set Up a Learning Center?

The organization and setup of learning centers are keys to developing a successful program in your classroom. Where and how you place your centers is important, remembering that they must be useable within your classroom. They may be set up on walls, in corners, behind partitions, on tables, on desks, or even in storage bins. Some centers may require an arrangement of equipment and materials where there is a water source, electrical outlet, or a special light. Wall space around a room is often a good place to set up learning centers. With such an arrangement, students are spread out around a room, so crowding doesn't take place. Flexibility is your most important asset in setting up centers.

How Do I Use a Learning Center?

Your first job is to introduce the learning center to your students. Let them know what the centers are for and how to use and take care of them, including cleaning up. This should be repeated every time new centers are introduced. Plan to spend some time at the beginning of each month explaining the proper procedures to follow at the centers. It may be helpful to post procedures and rules near each center. Some general rules include the following:

1. Use only one center at a time.
2. Put finished activities away before leaving.
3. Keep voices at an appropriate level.
4. Be careful with materials and equipment.
5. When finished, quietly return to your seat.

Introduction *(cont.)*

In *Learning Centers for Intermediate Classrooms*, the following learning centers are introduced:

Language Arts

Here, students have an opportunity to reinforce reading skills, enjoy literature, create a classroom newsletter, and write book reports, journals, poetry, and experience other forms of creative written expression. Allow for space to write and to create. Provide good books, writing materials, and plenty of filing systems that are well labeled.

Math

Students will reinforce math skills as they play games, solve puzzles, create measurement systems, and explore manipulatives. Provide a calculator, a stack of scratch paper, measuring devices, and counters such as beans, disks, etc.

Science

The science center will provide students with opportunities for hands-on science as they explore scientific experiments and learn about the sea, animals, and weather. The science center will require a variety of materials, from eye droppers to table salt. This will also be the place where you can display autumn leaves, seed pods, or the snake skin you found while camping last summer. Be sure to stock the science center with lots of books and reference volumes.

Social Studies

Finding out more about the world we live in, the people in our communities, and how we get along highlight this center. Be sure to include a globe and an atlas in this center, along with some historical objects, posters, and interesting inventions.

Games and Puzzles

At this center, students can play games that reinforce skills, challenge each other and themselves, and solve various kinds of puzzles. Provide scratch paper, reference volumes, lots of pens and pencils, and brightly colored posters.

Technology

Students will incorporate different software applications to reinforce their writing, math, and creative skills. They will have an opportunity to integrate concepts and skills from language arts, math, science, and social studies with their developing computer skills. There will also be activities directly tied to help students explore the Internet.

Overview

How to Use the Sections in This Book

Language Arts

The Language Arts section (pages 21–62) includes a variety of activities to reinforce language skills beginning with A New Product! (page 22). If your students have already learned about brainstorming, this will give them an opportunity to put the method into practice as they invent new products to market. You may wish to brainstorm ideas for products as a whole class first to inspire your students. This activity has been designed for individual work, but it will also work well with partners. Be sure to stock the learning centers with plenty of materials for students to use in their marketing campaigns. Decorate the classroom with posters, and if you wish, you may want to extend the activity by having students present oral commercials (live or videotaped).

For the Interviews (page 24) have students first go to the learning center alone to create a list of questions. Students will meet in pairs for their interviews and then work alone again to write their stories. You may wish to have examples of published interviews and bibliographies to inspire the young journalists. You may also want to compile the classroom interviews and make a classroom book with student profiles.

There are many ways to adapt the Editing (pages 25 and 26) section to meet your students' needs. You may wish to simply post the information in the center as a helpful reference. Alternatively, you may wish to create packets with the editing information and allow each student an opportunity to review the material and practice editing (see pages 27 and 28 for editing practice work sheets). This activity may be incorporated into a Writer's Workshop as students learn to edit each others' work.

You can turn a writing center into a newspaper office with the Class Newsletter activity (pages 29–31). Post the list of assigned duties in the center and rotate so that students each get a turn to do a variety of jobs throughout the school year. Place a file or box in the center into which contributing writers will place their submissions. Meet with editors from time to time to go over submitted material and to create the weekly or monthly newsletter. You may wish to add some art supplies to the center so that the newspaper can be visually appealing with art and illustrations. If you have access to a scanner or photo program, you may be able to add photos to your newsletter as well.

In the Creative Writing activities, you will find several pages that contain the guidelines for a variety of literary forms. You may make copies of these pages and file them under each genre in a special Creative Writing file in the center. Then you will be able to post the day's Creative Writing assignment, and students will be able to check and see how it is done, get inspired, and get to work. This file may also be used with other activities such as the class newsletter, a creative writing journal that publishes student work, or even to create letters or cards for special occasions. Keep the file stocked so that curious and interested students can take copies for their own use when they feel inspired.

The Story Starters (pages 37 and 38) are very useful. You may wish to simply post them in the writing center to inspire any student faced with a blank page, or you may wish to have

Overview *(cont.)*

all students use it for that day's writing center assignment. Another idea would be to cut them apart and place them in a slot, box, or envelope in the center so that each student can draw one for his or her story. The Story Scramble Cards (pages 39–42) may be cut out and placed into three separate containers (boxes, hats, envelopes, etc.) Each student selects a main character, a setting, and a situation to develop. He or she will then write a short story or a newspaper article based on the cards that are drawn. This activity may be completed individually or in pairs. The cards may also be used as story starter inspirations at any time.

Students will have the opportunity to exercise their creativity with Metaphors (page 43). You may wish to introduce the topic as a whole class before making the exercise available in the writing center. Encourage students to incorporate metaphors into their writing. Similarly, students will practice writing similes in I Feel As Silly As… (page 44). When each student has had the opportunity to create similes, you may want to collect the responses into a class book, post them on a bulletin board, or have the students share them orally in class.

The Letter Writing activities on pages 45–47 will introduce students to the proper format of letters. Once they are confident letter writers, you may wish to have them write letters to their favorite authors or become pen pals with students in a different class in another part of the country or the world. Posting the Pen Pal Pointers in the writing center will be especially helpful.

The Journals activities (pages 48 and 49) begin with a blank journal page to get students started. Additionally, you may wish to make copies and distribute the Journal Starts (page 49) or staple it to the inside cover of their journals. Allow students to keep their journals in a special place in the writing center and have students write in them regularly. Give credit for participation, not content of journals. If your students often have trouble with journal topics, you may wish to use the starters one at a time and have all students write to the same cue. Brainstorm as a class for more starter ideas and keep them in the writing center.

The Vocabulary, Spelling, and Punctuation activities are fun and challenging. Make only one or two copies of the Vocabulary Concentration game (pages 50 and 51). Laminate the cards and place them in a folder or box in the writing center. Then students may play the game by themselves or with a partner. You may also choose to make a copy for each student. To expand, create a file so that students can submit unusual words they run across in their reading. From time to time, add cards and definitions that the students have submitted to keep the game challenging. Similarly, your students will increase their dictionary and spelling skills with Spelling Quest (page 52), a challenging word hunt. Students may do the quest individually or with partners. To create even more of a challenge, invite students to use the dictionary to come up with new quests. In order to encourage students to use the dictionary, you will find on page 53 a form for the writing center dictionary. When students find a word that is unfamiliar to them, they can fill in the form, submit their page, and eventually find it published in the center dictionary. Be sure to leave the ever growing dictionary in a prominent place in the center so students can look at its pages often.

Punctuation Concentration (pages 54–56) is a game for two players (or more, if your center can handle more.) Players match the unpunctuated sentence cards with the correct punctuation. Their discussions of correct punctuation will reinforce learning as they play. This game can be played as a matching game for one or two.

Book reports will always be an important part of the curriculum. On page 57, you will find Getting Ideas. This page can be posted in the writing center, or each student may be given a copy. In addition, you may wish to have a brainstorming session with your students for additional book report ideas. Students will have an opportunity to respond to literature at an emotional and intellectual level when they complete You Choose! (page 58). This activity may be correlated with journal activities as well. To expand on this type of activity, keep a file full of student literature journals in the center. When in the center, students may write their feelings and responses to the books they are reading as they read them. Many stories include interesting animals as characters. In some stories, the animals are simply providing atmosphere or acting as part of the background. In other stories, the animals are an integral part of the plot and have almost human characteristics. With the Animal or Human? activity (page 59), students will be provided with the opportunity to analyze the animal characters and compare them to human characters as they report on a book they have read. The Sequel (page 60) inspires students to plan a continuation of the book they have just read. How would they continue the story? This writing activity requires thought and will likely cause students to look at plots a little more closely in the future.

Students will strengthen research skills while writing a book report when they complete Finding Facts (page 61), which will have them using various resources to learn facts about the setting of their story. This activity may be joined with a geography or social studies unit. Mapping the Matter (page 62) also combines geography with language arts. In this activity, students draw a map to show where the events in the story take place. This activity could be combined with the Finding Facts activity, but it is especially suitable for books that have a fictional or fantasy setting. This activity is also good for those books which never exactly state the setting other than "a forest" or "a large and cavernous, old mansion full of dark hallways, and secret doors…."

Math

The Math section (pages 63–103) begins with a favorite math topic—money. The Value of Art (pages 64 and 65) is a good activity for students who groan when they are told to take their math books out. This activity combines creative expression with math and reinforces the addition of monetary sums painlessly. You may wish to display the results of the students' money math art on a special bulletin board. Strike It Rich! (page 66) continues the money theme as students work the math to learn who appeared on the $100,000 bill. Change for Fifty Cents (page 67) is a fun yet challenging math money activity. Students may work in pairs or individually to find as many combinations as they can. It may be helpful to use real or play money to manipulate or duplicate the coins on page 64 and cut out for student use. Students will determine the value of various words with The Value of Words (page 68) using a code wherein each letter of the alphabet is assigned a dollar value. To expand this activity, students can purchase and sell words using play money as a whole class activity. Have students create their own codes and create problems for other students to solve. They can tell the dollar amount of a word and tell what some of the letters are and let classmates try to figure out what the word is.

With the Word Problem activities on page 69 and 70, students will solve and write their own word problems. Make many copies of the word problems form and post word problem examples in the math center. Add a box or file so that students may deposit their word problems for other students to solve and/or try to solve the word problems written by their classmates. Cookie Math (page 71) is word problem activity that students will find both challenging and appetizing. You may want to add a class math activity by baking chocolate chip cookies together.

Measuring the ingredients for making the cookies is a good transition into the Measurement activities (pages 72–78), which begins with Metric System on page 72. This activity introduces students to the metric system as they measure and record common items that will be in the center or on their own bodies. To expand this activity, add more items to measure outside of the center in the classroom, on the playground, or in their homes. The Measurement activities continue with an activity which has students measuring the same items with the Customary System (page 73). Again, expand by adding additional items to be measured. Measurement concepts will be reinforced as students complete New System (page 74). Here, students will create their own unit of measurement and, once again, go about the business of measuring familiar items. This activity would tie in well with a whole class look at how early measuring systems began. On page 75 students will compare all three systems as a culminating activity for the unit on measurement.

Measuring Without a Ruler (page 76) may be used as a poster for the math center. In addition, it may be helpful to make enough copies for each student to keep. The measurement unit may be expanded by having each student use these measuring "tools" to measure and record various items around the house. The results would make an interesting bulletin board display. In addition, students may be inspired to create a measurement lesson to teach to younger students. For a challenging finale to the center's unit on measurement, have students take the Measurement Challenge on pages 77 and 78. You may prefer that students work alone or with a partner.

It is only natural that as students complete a unit on measurement, they will be ready to learn to draw to scale with the Drawing to Scale activity (page 79). Students will begin to see the patterns to be found in numbers when they do the Prime Time activity, based on the Sieve of Eratosthenes (page 80). Use the Tangrams activity (pages 81–83) in the math center, and students will make connections between shapes and math in creative ways. This will prepare them for geography as well as many other math subjects. The Symmetry activities (pages 84 and 85) bridge the gap between map and art, thereby allowing the more visually-oriented students to make math connections. These are independent activities. To extend the activity, have students create their own symmetry challenges for other students to complete.

The activities in the Computing unit (pages 86–93) begin with a series of creative addition, subtraction, multiplication, and division activities on pages 86–89. Because these activities approach math skills in a new and different way, they will reinforce student learning. Calculator Fun activities (pages 90 and 91) are challenging, creative, and fun. Students will not be aware that they are strengthening math skills as they use calculators to solve the word problems. For even more of a challenge, invite students to create their own Calculator Fun problems. The Money Maze (page 92) will reinforce the math concepts introduced in previous money-related activities. Science and math are combined in Energy Facts (page 93). To extend this activity, have students choose one of the science facts they discovered while doing the activity and research for more information. Students may also create their own facts on subjects they choose. Your students can test their math knowledge with the Math Facts activities (pages 94–97). You may wish to use the questions as research prompts or cut the questions out and place them in a box. Have students draw one each time they enter the math center and give them a deadline for finding the answer and reporting it.

The Graphing activities (pages 98 and 99) will enable your students to understand the concepts of graphing while using a familiar subject—themselves. You may wish to choose one or two of the subjects at a time and have each student fill in a brief form in the learning center or place a write-on board or chalkboard in the center with columns so that students can list their eye color and other facts in the appropriate column. Individual students or pairs of students may compile the information and create graphs. Have them make their graphs large and colorful for classroom display.

You will need to place an old telephone in the math center for the What Is the Message? (page 100) activity. Students will be decoding "telephone numbers" to find words related to the people on the list. This activity reinforces social study skills as well as math. To expand this activity, have students create their own codes in the form of "telephone numbers." Scrambled Math (page 101) will challenge students to remember math terms that they have learned as they unscramble the words. Math True or False (pages 102) will challenge students' math knowledge. Have students research a topic with that they are not familiar with and report to the class, orally or in writing. How Many? (page 103) is a fun yet challenging activity. To extend this activity, have students research through encyclopedias to find more "how manys." They can write "how many" questions on one side of index cards and responses on the backs. As a whole class divided into teams, play the "How Many?" game once students have had time to research and write questions.

Science

The Science section (pages 104–139) begins with a form that can be used throughout the year when doing experiments with the whole class, teams, or individuals. Make plenty of copies for the science center. The first experiment in the Experiments unit is The Sensational Submarine (page 106). Depending on the abilities of your students and on how much work they have already completed with science experiments, you may wish to demonstrate this one to the whole class and then leave the materials and work sheets in the center. If students have had some experience, they will enjoy this experiment as an individual activity or working in pairs. To extend, have students make predictions before they try the experiment.

Rambunctious Raisins! (page 109) is another experiment that students may do as individuals or in pairs. Again, depending on your students' abilities, you may wish to demonstrate this experiment to the whole class first. A class discussion after the experiment is a good idea as well. The experiment You're Full of Hot Air! (page 111) requires a hairdryer as the source of hot air. Students will construct "balloons" from tissue paper. These constructions will need a day to dry before they continue with the experiment.

The Sea Life activity (pages 112 and 113) will offer students an opportunity to research a topic about life under the sea. They need not be limited to the questions posed in the activity. The Sea Life Phyla Chart may be used as a poster and/or as a supplement to students' folders for that unit of study. The Create a Zoo activity (pages 114 and 115) may be as ambitious as you would like it to be. In any case, the activity will take more than one session in the science center. Students will be designing a zoo to meet the specifications of the mayor of the city.

In the Zoology unit (pages 114–117), Native Australian Animals (page 116) is a fun word game that will introduce students to the unusual wildlife of Australia. Challenge students to find pictures of each of the animals in encyclopedias, on the Internet, or in other resources. To extend this activity, have each student choose one of the animals to write a one- to two-page, illustrated report containing interesting facts about the animal. Students can test their knowledge of the names of different kinds of animals and their group names with the activity, Animal Families and Groups (page 117). You may wish to supply a resource so students can look up the terms that are unfamiliar to them. To extend, challenge students to think of other animals for which they may find group names.

You may wish to post the Amazing Weather Facts (page 118) in the center as inspiration, or you may prefer to cut the amazing facts apart and post one per week in the science center. Encourage students to find more amazing weather facts and create a bulletin board to display the amazing things they found. There are many excellent books and videos on the phenomenon of weather that you may want to add to the center to satisfy the curiosity of your young scientists. Have students each choose a weather topic, such as tornadoes, hurricanes, hail, the weather on another planet, lightning, etc., and prepare a report. Similarly, Alaskan Weather (page 119) will interest any student not living in Alaska. (If you are teaching in Alaska, use the page as a model and study a state with higher temperatures overall, for the contrast.) Students are likely to be more thoughtful about temperatures after completing this activity. To challenge students, have them look in an atlas to find the lowest and highest temperatures on Earth for each month of the year. Students will create hot air spirals with Create the Wind (page 120). You may wish to demonstrate in advance or let the students take the materials provided and, individually or in pairs, discover for themselves. Be sure to discuss the results and their responses. High or Low? (page 121) offers students the opportunity to create a barometer. After they have completed this activity, they will have a better understanding of the daily weather report and may even be able to forecast weather themselves.

The Science Quest activities (pages 123–130) will introduce students to amazing and little known facts about science that are guaranteed to motivate them to want to know more.

Overview (cont.)

Encourage students to choose a fact from the trivia activities (or the true or false activities) to research more fully. Have them prepare oral reports to present to the class. To extend, videotape the reports or create a science show to present to students in other classrooms. The Scientific Names activity (page 128) will familiarize students with some of the inventors and discoveries in the world of science. When they have completed the activity, they will understand why we use the terms watt, volt, etc. Again, this activity is a good springboard toward further research.

Science Clues (page 129) is a word game with clues to find science words. Students will have fun solving the puzzle and not realize that their knowledge of science is being reinforced. Science ABCs (page 130) is a formidable activity to complete. The directions state that students should not use a dictionary, but if you wish, you can provide resources, depending upon the skill level of your students. You may wish to play "21 Questions" with the class prior to introducing this activity to be sure that students understand the concept of animal, vegetable, or mineral. This activity may be completed by individual or paired students.

Laminate and cut out the cards for Matching the Sciences (pages 131–133). Place the cards in the science center for students to play by themselves or with a partner. Have students create additional cards to make the game more challenging and interesting. Similarly, Insect Bingo (page 134) and Vertebrate and Invertebrate Animals (page 138) will test your students' knowledge while making science more fun and visually stimulating as students learn to identify different animals.

Social Studies

The Social Studies section (pages 140–176) begins with historical names. Famous Names (page 141) is an activity that may require research for most students so be sure to provide resource materials in the center. Inventors and Their Inventions (page 142) is the perfect complement to a unit on inventions. To extend this activity, have students spend some time brainstorming and developing their own inventions. Introduce the students to the famous invention of the Braille Code with Louis Braille's Code (page 143). After solving the codes in the activity, students can use the code to write their own message. If possible, obtain a sample of a page from a book in Braille to place in the center so that students realize that it is a code that one feels with the fingers. Have them try to identify the letters without using their eyes. If you are unable to obtain a sample, you can create a sample using thick paper such as watercolor paper. Use an object to make impressions (such as a straight or hat pin with a ball at the end or any other object that is handy). Let students know that they can find Braille in unusual places (such as in elevators) so they should be observant and report their findings.

Presidential First Names (page 145) will reinforce history studies. This activity will be difficult for some students. If your students need some assistance, you can post pictures of the presidents in the social studies center or create flash cards for student use. Famous Women (page 146) is an activity that will introduce students to the contributions of several famous and admirable women in history. Be sure that students have an opportunity to check

© Teacher Created Materials, Inc.

and correct their answers in order to foster learning. Famous People (page 147) is another formidable activity. Provide clues or answer the first question with the whole class if your students need a little help getting started. Make the answer key available for self-checking.

Students will be introduced to the subject of geography with Countries of South America (page 148). With only vowels as a clue, students will need an atlas or globe to figure out which countries are listed. Once they have completed this activity, they may know more about this part of the world than they would have previously, as they will have looked closely to locate the countries. Encourage their curiosity about these countries by providing additional resources in the center. Once students have located the South American countries, they are ready for the challenge found in Test Your Map Skills (pages 149–151). In this case, they will be discovering interesting facts about the United States as they find the answers by looking at a map. In addition to the map on page 151, you may want to also provide an atlas and other resources in the center.

Matching World Capitals (pages 152–155) is a game that may be played with two or more students in the center. If played with just two students, have each student be his or her own "team." The game may also be played as a simple matching game when only one student plays. Students are introduced to longitude and latitude with the activity Where Is It? (pages 156 and 157). When students have completed this activity, extend it by having them create their own Where Is It? pages. As a whole class or as an individual activity, you many enjoy creating treasure hunts where students search the globe according to degrees north, degrees west, etc., until they find the location and win the prize.

Students will delve more fully into history beginning with Black History Trivia (page 158). Provide plenty of resources for students to research the answers to the questions. When all have completed this activity, have each student choose one of the 15 subjects and write a report or prepare a speech on the topic. Hang a calendar in the social studies center and add plenty of references for the activity on American Holidays Trivia (page 159). In addition, students can also research the origins of the holidays mentioned in the activity and other holidays and write a few paragraphs describing how they began. Have them add an illustration and create a visual display of the origins of many different holidays or, if you prefer, save their work and add the appropriate pieces to the large display calendar each month.

Students will be further tested by Social Studies Trivia and More Social Studies Trivia (pages 160 and 161). Once students are familiar with the format, have them research and create their own social studies trivia questions. Have them write each question on one side of an index card and the answer on the other side. When you have collected enough cards, have students create a Trivial Pursuit-type game board with playing pieces. Play the game in pairs at the center.

Just for fun, you may want to provide props, or at least magazine photos, to go along with This Map Is Making Me Hungry! on page 162. A chili or two, a bottle of mustard, and maybe some cheese and chocolate kisses will help illustrate the fact that we live in a delicious world. Also provide an atlas or a globe for your hungry globetrotters. To extend this activity, provide a large wall map of the world and have students place push pins or tacks in the locations. If you want to take this one step further, glue a small picture of a bottle of mustard, a hot dog, etc., to the top of each push pin or tack.

Place Names of the World (page 163) is a challenging and thought-provoking activity that will prompt students to not take city names for granted and make them wonder about the history of the cities they encounter. Be sure to provide the appropriate reference resources and have a class discussion after the students have completed this assignment. Students may be surprised to discover that states have nicknames. The Nicknames and Capitals activity (page 164) will have students researching to find the nicknames of each state along with its capital. To study further, have students choose five states and find out the reason each has a nickname. Puzzled About the States? (page 165) is a visual activity that will test students to identify the states when seen in an entirely new way. They may also use a map on page 151 to make their own puzzles.

In the Families and Friends unit, My Family Tree (pages 170–173) will help students understand where their families come from and trace their family history to find out about their family lineage. As each student delves into their family's history, some may discover that there is part of their heritage woven into the workmanship of a family quilt that has been passed on from one generation to the next. In the final activity in the Social Studies section, students will go to the center to find a Patchwork Quilt Kit (pages 174–176). Each student will create his or her own patchwork square from construction paper and glue. Suggest that they may want to choose specific colors or shapes to represent things that are meaningful to them. When they have completed their squares, they will write their names on the backs of their squares. These may be collected and pieced together on a bulletin board or bound in a classroom book. You may want to laminate each square for durability. To further expand on this activity, have students create multiple squares in order to make a larger pattern similar to an actual quilt. If you or a parent can demonstrate quilt-making, have a guest speaker/demonstrator visit the classroom. You may even wish to create an actual quilt in class. The simplest way would be to give each student a square of plain muslin and have him or her decorate it with fabric markers. Collect them and have a parent or volunteer stitch them together. Add backing and fill and then stitch the quilt front to back. To keep the fill materials from bunching, tie or stitch the quilt at regular intervals. Take photos of the quilt for each student and present it to the principal or a nursing home in the area.

Games and Puzzles

The Games and Puzzles section (pages 177–219) begins with humor. Students are given examples of various forms of written jokes and puns and are encouraged to follow suit and write their own. Create a class joke book and accept submissions. Edit for content before publishing them in the book. When students tackle Presidential Stumpers (page 179), remind them that if they take it too seriously, it will stump them. The first one, which has been done as an example, should give them the idea. Challenge students to create their own stumpers on the topics of their own choice. Letter Answers and More Letter Answers (pages 180 and 181) will stump students in a similar fashion. Provide answer keys so they can check their answers.

Overview (cont.)

Which Came First? (page 182) will challenge their knowledge and sense of history. Provide resource materials for students who need to find the answers. To expand this activity, create a wall chart with moveable sentence strips. Have students place items in order of chronology while in the center. They may move things around if they are not sure, or if they learn chronology while in the center. Your students may be surprised to discover how many states end in the letter "A." The word search activity, States Ending in "A" (page 183), may be challenging enough, but if you would like to make it more challenging, omit the list of 21 states before making copies.

There are several activities that give students the opportunity to crack and create codes, beginning with Morse Code on page 184. Provide plenty of copies of Morse Code for student use in the center. As a supplemental class activity, you may wish to provide a recording so that students will be able to hear what Morse Code sounds like. If you can't find a recording, you may wish to tap out the letters and have the students learn to tap them, too, in unison. Code activities continue with Coded Message (page 185). This activity will also require some research to complete so be sure to provide plenty of research materials in the center. Proverbial Codes and More Proverbial Codes (pages 186 and 187) are fun code-breaking activities that use familiar proverbs. As an extension to this activity, have students brainstorm a list of familiar phrases and then they can remove words and create codes for them. Have them exchange papers and decode each other's work. Communicating in Code (page 188) introduces students to additional forms of codes, including sign language. Make plenty of copies of this page for students to use in other activities. To expand, you may want to discuss with students the use of the Navajo language during World War II. Find books on the topic and explain to them that intelligence officers used the Navajo language as a code because it was a language that they were certain the Nazis would not be able to comprehend or figure out. Introduce your students to a few simple Navajo phrases. You may also wish to compare Navajo to Polynesian languages, such as Hawaiian, to note how they appear to have some similarities. Students may be curious about why this is the case. In the second part of Communicating in Code, students will create a code and write a paragraph using their own code. Be sure that they keep a clear copy of their created code.

Creativity is encouraged with the Wacky Words activities on pages 190–194. In addition to an interesting display, students may play a password kind of game as they try to guess which of the definitions is the correct one. Students will increase their vocabularies painlessly as they complete this activity. To extend, have students find additional wacky words and create an illustrated wacky words book for the center. Rhyming Word Pairs (pages 191 and 192) are activities that your students are certain to enjoy even as they groan over the word plays. Post a write-on/write-off board in the center so students can write any new rhyming word pairs that they may create while solving the puzzle. Be sure to collect their ideas into a file to create new word pair fun.

Palindrome fun begins on page 193. In the center post some palindromes as examples, such as wow, toot, and even, "Madam, I'm Adam." Once students have the idea, they will enjoy palindromes. Be sure to have the answer key available in the center for checking answers. For a challenging word puzzle, give your students Palindrome Word Find (page 194).

Overview *(cont.)*

The literary matching game, Match That Author! (pages 195 and 196), can be played be played individually or with a partner. To extend this game, add additional cards, especially focusing on authors and books which the class has studied. Throughout the year, you may want to have students create one author and one book card for each book they read. Collect these for more challenging matching games which may also inspire additional reading. Crazy, Mixed-Up Sentences (pages 197–199) is a fun activity for students of all ages. Students may manipulate the cards to create surprising sentences. Partners can each provide one or two of the parts of a sentence before seeing what has been chosen by the other and then put the sentence together. You may wish to affix the sentence parts to magnetic strips so students can create crazy sentences on a filing cabinet or a cookie sheet. To expand, have students create additional strips.

The Economics Game (pages 200–206) is a good supplemental to any unit on economics, the Great Depression, or personal finance. It may be played as described, with four or five players in a group, or it may be played as a matching game by an individual student. The game may be played even if you do not have the class study economics because students can learn a great deal of economic vocabulary. Bring in a game of Monopoly® as a related activity for students.

The Creative Puzzlers (pages 207–211) begin with Color This Design (page 207). This activity appears to be pretty simple so you may want to warn your students to read the directions and think it through before they start coloring. Display the finished products and discuss the differences and similarities in the students' work. I've Been Framed! (page 208), Hidden Meanings (pages 209 and 210), and Word Chains (page 211) are fun for children and adults alike. Students may work alone or with partners. You may wish to add puzzle books to the center that contain these kinds of creative work puzzles, and you will definitely want to encourage your students to create their own.

Students' computation skills will be exercised as they work with the Math Squares on page 212. Laminate the squares for durability, if you wish, and place them in the games and puzzles center. You may want to make enough copies so that each student can have his or her own set of Math Squares. Students may work alone to line up the squares; however, two students can play a kind of dominoes game with the squares. To challenge students, have each student create their own math squares, using the pattern of four squares across and four down. A game for two players can be found on page 213, Factors and Multiples. Be sure to make lots of copies as students will not want to stop at one round of this one, and their math skills will be strengthened as they play.

In the Puzzling Math unit, Improper Fraction Mix-Up (page 214) will test students' understanding of fractions to unscramble the hidden message. Skills with fractions will further be reinforced when your students play Fractured Fractions (page 215). This game is played in pairs so you may wish to rotate students through in such a way that they each have an opportunity to play against or with many other classmates. You may expand this activity by creating a Fractured Fractions tournament by having older students teach younger students how to play. Students will enjoy playing Close the Box (page 216) and may not realize that they are strengthening their math skills as they play. The game may be played with partners, or if the center is conducive to it, more players can play. You will need to place copies of the game, dice, and counters (such as beans, disks, etc.) in the center in order for the game to be played. A pair of students in the center can play Decimal Derby (page 217). Be sure to make plenty of copies of the activity sheet as students will want to play the games more than once, and they will reinforce decimal skills in the process. You may also wish to place a calculator in the center for accurate checking of answers. Spaceship Flip, a geometry game on page 218, is also designed for a pair of students. You may wish to make the spinner ahead of time or provide one copy of the game (two of the spaceship) for each partnership and allow them to prepare the game for play. Place materials, such as pencils, paper clips, markers, and crayons, so students can make a spinner and fill their spaceships.

Technology

In the Technology section, a brief introduction is provided about using the Internet in your classroom. A list of Internet Safety Rules for Students (page 222) is provided and should be discussed with the entire class before starting any Internet related activities in the Technology section. This section should be used by teachers to incorporate different software applications into the classroom in language arts, science, math, and social studies. Some activities are specifically designed to incorporate the Internet and students. Researching on the World Wide Web and others provide teachers with Web sites that they can use to gather more information about the topic or activity. Many activities in this section suggest what type of software should be used by students.

This section begins with language arts activities. Create Your Own Advertisement (page 224) lets students use a drawing program or word processing software to create an advertisement for a school event. In Writing Good Descriptions (pages 225–227) students will be able to create a character for a story. To expand this activity, encourage students to write a story about their new character. More writing and creativity can further be enhanced by Computer Poetry (pages 228–232) which introduces students to different types of poetry and provides examples of each one. This activity lets students learn more about different word processing software and adding clip art from CD-ROMs.

The science activities in the Technology section begin with Properties of Matter (page 233). In this activity students determine whether different things are solid, liquid, or gas and then make a brochure explaining the different states of matter. The brochure may be created in either a program with special fold capabilities for brochures or a regular word processing program. (See the activity for details.) The topic about the characteristics of matter are further enhanced by Investigating Matter—Making Models (page 236) in which students design and create their own atomic models using a drawing program. There are Internet sites listed in the activity that will offer you and your students information and examples about atoms. The Nine Planets (page 238) activity also provides the opportunity for students to learn more information from the Internet. Each student will choose a planet to study and gather information about it. They will then type their information and add clip art to post in the center bulletin board or to add to a classroom book about the nine planets.

Overview (cont.)

A Year in the Life of a Tree (pages 239–246) is a *Kid Pix* project for students to complete on the computer. This activity is designed for students to follow the life of a deciduous tree through one full school year. If this activity won't work as a learning center project, it can be part of your science unit on plants and trees. In either case, students will increase computer skills as well as knowledge of trees and seasons as they complete this project.

The math activities begin with The Fraction Machine (pages 247 and 248). Using a drawing program, students will create fractions that reinforce their growing knowledge about fractions and how parts add up to make a whole. Fractions in a Box (pages 249 and 250) expands on the math concepts introduced in The Fraction Machine by letting the students create different fraction boxes. In Mystery Squares (pages 251 and 252), students will create their own mystery squares which they can share with their classmates. This activity involves a drawing program that students will use to create their Mystery Squares. Similarly, It All Adds Up (pages 253 and 254) incorporates the use of a drawing program for students to create currency on the computer to discover how many combinations will add up to a $1.00. This activity can be done individually or in pairs. Students will write down their results on a chart and discuss their results. As an extension, students can make this activity a contest between teams to see who can list more combinations in the shortest amount of time.

Not Your Average Board Game (pages 255–257) is a math game that challenges students to create a board game that they will use to practice finding averages. This is an activity that has specific directions on how the board game should be created and how it should be played. You may want to also use this activity as a prototype to create other math concept games that will help students have fun while practicing their math skills.

The Social Studies unit begins with Current Events (pages 258–260). For this activity, students become reporters and write news stories which they will present in class. This activity incorporates the Internet to help students gather information about their news story. Similarly, The Olympics (pages 261–263) is an activity that lets students research the history of the Olympics using different reference sources and the Internet. This activity can be incorporated into a unit of study about the Olympics and the different locations where past Olympics have been held. Egyptian Facts from the Internet (pages 264 and 265) also helps students delve into the culture and history of a different nation—Egypt. Students will use specific Internet addresses to gather information and create their own fact sheet about Egypt.

Some students may want to create a travel brochure for Egypt with the activity, Welcome to My Travel Agency (pages 266–270). This activity is designed for *Kid Pix* so students can create their own travel brochure about a country. Students will be choosing a destination and enticing others to visit by promoting its features. Have plenty of resources on hand so students may research the details of their destination. The finished products will make a wonderful display in the classroom. The activity includes some sample pages of what type of information and clip art could be incorporated.

Language Arts

A New Product!

New products are being created all the time. Now it's your turn to think of a new product and sell it. First, you will need to brainstorm for some ideas. Your product could be a food, a hair product, a cleaning aid, a new kind of shoe, or whatever you can imagine.

In the space below, write the advertisement that will promote your new product. Be sure to make people excited about your new product, tell them why they should buy it, and where to find it. Next, create a poster to show what your product will look like. You can use the back of this page to make a sketch. Make your poster colorful and attractive so that people will want to buy your product. Use the checklist on page 23 to check your work.

A New Product! *(cont.)*

Advertising Campaign Checklist

The Writing

❑ I have painted a picture with my words.

❑ I have told the reader why he or she should buy my product.

❑ I have explained what it is and why it is important.

❑ I have told where to buy it.

❑ I have written a paragraph that will make people excited about my product.

❑ I have rewritten my ad, revising and improving it.

The Art

❑ I have made my product appealing by presenting it in eye-catching colors.

❑ I have designed a poster that makes my product appear exciting.

❑ I have presented my product clearly in my poster.

Interviews

Interviews and profiles of famous people are a popular form of journalism. You will be interviewing a classmate, and, in turn, your classmate will interview you. First, make a list of interesting questions. The usual questions like, where were you born, what is your favorite color and how many brothers and sisters do you have are fine but think of some unusual questions, too. After you have plenty of questions (try to have about 10–15), get together with a partner and take turns interviewing each other. Write the responses quickly and, after the interview is over, take your notes and write a story about your partner and include the most interesting facts. Your interview should be at least one page. When you are finished, your teacher may want to collect the interviews and put them into a classroom book, complete with a photograph. He or she may also ask you to introduce your partner to the rest of the class by sharing some of the things you learned in your interview.

Here are some interview questions to add to the ones that you come up with.

- If you were an animal, what animal would you be?

- What is your favorite season of the year, and why?

- If you could paint your entire house inside and out with one color, what would it be and why?

- When you have children, what will you name them?

- If you could only have one book for the rest of your life, what book would you choose?

- If you were a car, what car would you be?

- What food do you hate the most?

- Do you like to climb trees? Why or why not?

- What is the most unusual place you have ever been?

- What is the most embarrassing thing that has ever happened to you?

- What chore do you dislike the most?

- What famous person would you like to meet?

- Who do you look like the most, your mom or your dad?

- What is your favorite song and why?

- What would you like to change about yourself?

- Do you think you will be famous some day? For what?

Editing

Editing is an important job. Your writing will be better if you learn to edit, and you can help others improve their writing with your editing help. Asking a friend to edit your stories is also important because he or she may find things that you missed. After you have completed the activities on pages 27 and 28, trade stories with a partner to edit each other's work. Use the checklist below, and the editing marks on page 26 to help you remember how to edit.

Steps Toward Good Self-Editing

1. Don't worry about perfection on a first draft.

When you first sit down to write, just let it all come out. Don't worry about how good it is or whether you have used the perfect verb. Just get it all down before you forget it, and then put it away until later.

2. Read aloud what you have written.

Reading aloud what you have written lets you hear it in much the same way someone else will read it. Is it smooth? Does it say what you want it to say? Have you included the facts you want to include? If it's a story, do your characters seem like real people?

3. Start cutting and rewriting.

Use active verbs. Cut out verbs which begin with *was, were, is, had been, seemed to be,* and *did.* Don't use the word *that* if you can get by without it. Don't use verbs with *-ly* words. Be specific.

Instead of saying

Marilyn was climbing slowly up the steep hill. She was panting.

write

Marilyn struggled up the hill, lungs gasping, heart pounding.

4. When writing a story, use good dialogue.

Let the reader get to know a character by what that character says and by what other characters say to him or her or about him or her.

5. Cut and rewrite some more.

Take out any word that doesn't have to be there. Don't say the same thing twice. Check for spelling and grammar mistakes. Spell checkers are helpful, but they will not tell you when you have used the wrong word: *here* for *hear, form* for *from,* for example.

6. Ask a friend to read what you have written.

Sometimes another person can see something that needs to be changed which you fail to see.

Editing *(cont.)*

Use this page as a reference when you revise and edit a story or article.

Editor's Mark	Meaning	Example
✗	Delete	My dog ~~done~~ came home.
≡	Capitalize	poison oak gives me a rash. ≡
/	Make lower case	That M̸ovie is my favorite.
∧	Add a word	cream Ice sundae ∧
RO	Run-on sentence	I fell down you helped me. RO
frag	Sentence fragment	Because we were late. frag
SP	Spelling error	SP Three little kitens sat in the tree.
∿	Reverse letters or words	My ⟨brother big⟩ is tall and skinny.
⊙	Add a period	I love books ⊙
∧̦	Add a comma	We ate chicken, potatoes ∧̦ and salad.
∨̓	Add an apostrophe	I'm in John's class.
❝ ❞	Add quotation marks	❝Come here! ❞my mother said.
¶	Begin new paragraph	"Help me with my homework," Mary pleaded.¶"No," her mother replied.
#	Make a space	# post office
⌢	Close the space	rain⌣bow
stet	Do not delete (let what was deleted remain)	stet The ~~strange~~ man shuffled along.

Editing *(cont.)*

Editing Practice

Edit the following Native American story. For help, you can refer to your chart of editor's marks.

this is a very sad story because it is about two people who love each other very much and want to marry but they have never been able to do so.

sun loves moon more than life itself he knows she is the most beautiful being ever seen on earth sun would give everything he has if only he could win her for his wife alas the one time he asked her to marry him she said oh yes i will marry you but there is one thing you must do first

anything sun answered i will do anything you say for i love you very much just tell me what it is

moon told him to prove your love for me you must bring me a gift that fits me exactly

what gift would you like me to bring

it can be anything to wear but it must fit me exactly moon replied.

time and time again sun comes with a gift for moon to wear but one time the gift is too small and the next time it is too large it is never exactly the right size this happens each time sun comes with a gift for moon to wear so on and on sun tries with gift after gift when you see sun crying you must know it is because he loves moon more than anything but he can never marry her

Editing *(cont.)*

More Editing Practice

Edit the following Native American Story. For help, you can refer to your chart of editor's marks.

one day turkey was walking on a trail through the woods when by chance he met terrapin turkey who wears a red flowing wattle and carries his head high in the air thinks he is better than other people when he saw terrapin with his slow clumsy gait and the hard shelled house he carries on his back he could not resist the opportunity to bring him down a peg or two

what on earth are you good for turkey asked in his usual snobbish way

i am good for many things terrapin replied i can beat you in a race

ha ha ha laughed turkey that is the silliest thing I have ever heard you beat me in a race ha ha ha

so they had a race they met at the edge of the village because all terrapins look alike in their shell houses terrapin was to carry a white feather in his mouth so he would be different from all the other terrapins they began

turkey did not know terrapin had a lot of friends and they all think alike and get along with each other at each hill a friend was waiting with a white feather in his mouth to carry on a relay to the end of the race meanwhile turkey walked slowly along sure he would win much to his surprise as he neared the finish line he saw terrapin crossing it he never figured out why can you

Class Newsletter

Your class will be publishing a newsletter to send to your family, the principal, and others. The newsletter will share news about what is going on in your classroom, and it will also be a place to publish your creative writing. There will be assigned positions on the newsletter staff. These will rotate so that everyone will have a turn. Everyone in the class, however, whether on the staff or not, will be a contributing writer.

In the writing center, there will be a file or a box into which you may place your contributions to the newsletter. Don't worry if your contribution does not appear in the very next newsletter. The hard news and assigned pieces always go in first. After that, the more creative pieces fill in. On page 31 or posted in the writing center, you will find a list of possible entries for the newsletter's creative writing file. You are not, however, limited to what is on the list. The teacher and the newsletter staff will review all submissions and decide which will fit best for each newsletter. On page 30 or posted in the writing center, you will find a list of the staff.

Class Newsletter *(cont.)*

Newsletter Staff _____

_____

_____

Editor in Chief _____

Assistant Editor _____

Creative Writing Editor _____

Assistant Creative Writing Editor _____

Art _____

_____

Reporters _____

_____

_____

Copy Editors _____

_____

_____

_____

_____

_____

_____

Class Newsletter *(cont.)*

Types of Possible Entries

Below are suggestions for the types of entries which can go into a class newsletter. As a group, discuss the merits of each type, and list any others of which you can think. Check the entries you wish to include in your class newsletter.

- ❏ Personal experience story
- ❏ Human interest story
- ❏ Poetry: haiku, cinquain, holiday, season, month, list, any topic
- ❏ Short story
- ❏ "My Favorite Animal"
- ❏ Movie/television/music/book reviews
- ❏ Cartoon/comic strips
- ❏ "The Most Interesting Person I've Ever Met"
- ❏ Letters to the editor, editorials
- ❏ Advice column
- ❏ Biographical feature
- ❏ "How to" article, such as "How I Budget My Allowance" or "How to Oil a Bike"
- ❏ School tips, such as "Organizing a Binder"
- ❏ Interesting facts in history
- ❏ Weird happenings, stranger than fiction
- ❏ Person of the Month
- ❏ Teacher of the Month
- ❏ (Other possibilities)

_____

_____

_____

_____

Writer's Guide

❏ *Personal Experience Story*

A personal experience story is a true story about something unusual that happened to you. It can be amazing or wonderful, scary or sad, or something which caused you to say to yourself, "Oh, yeah! Now I understand!"

Write a personal experience story. Write it in the *first person,* that is, using the pronoun "I." Use nouns, verbs, and adjectives which will make your story come "alive" for your reader. Allow your reader to see, smell, feel, and hear what happened. Always remember that **when you write, you write something for someone else to read. You want your story to be as clear as possible.**

Some suggestions for ways to begin your personal experience story are as follows:

- The funniest thing that ever happened to me was . . .

- I'll never forget the day that . . .

- Have you ever had a big surprise? I mean a REALLY big surprise? Well, I want to tell you about the biggest surprise I ever had. It was . . .

- I was so scared the day that . . .

Now, do you have a few ideas about how to begin your personal experience story? Good! Now you can get on with it!

❏ *Poetry*

There is a style or form of poetry to fit every taste. Some poems are formal with a specific rhyme scheme. A *limerick* is formal in the sense that it contains a definite number of lines (five), with a specific rhythm like these:

There once was a great reading class
That tried very hard, but alas,
The spring sun was shining,
And the students were pining
To run without shoes through the grass.

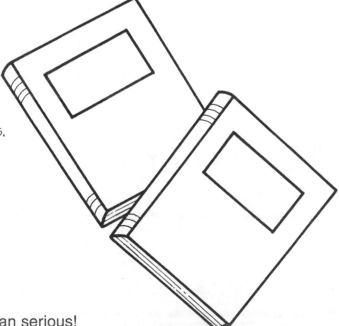

There once was a student in school
Who followed a practical rule:
She hid all her books
In crannies and nooks
And never ate bugs from a pool.

As you can see, *formal* doesn't necessarily mean serious!

Writer's Guide *(cont.)*

❏ *Poetry* *(cont.)*

Another kind of formal poem is the *haiku*, which contains three lines but does not rhyme. Traditional haiku is about nature or the seasons. This is an example of haiku.

> Clouds crossing the moon
> Catch its glow in their webbing,
> A vision in silver.

Strict haiku form also calls for the first line to have five syllables, the second line to have seven syllables, and the third line to have five syllables—17 syllables in all. You will notice that the third line of the above poem actually has six syllables, so it is close but not perfect.

> Leaves red, gold, and tawny　　　　　　Red, gold, and tawny
> Fall with the breezes,　　　　　　　　Leaves descend with the breezes
> And dance on the lawn.　　　　　　　And dance on the lawn.

How many syllables are in each of the lines in the above verses? Can you tell which example conforms to strict haiku form?

A kind of poem called a *cinquain* (from the French *cinq* for five) has five lines. Follow the form in the example below to write one kind of cinquain.

First line	Noun	*Kittens*
Second line.	Two adjectives	*Soft, furry*
Third line.	Three verb	*Tumbling, rolling, playing,*
Fourth line	Statement	*Get wrapped up in knitting yarn.*
Fifth line	Conclusion	*How will they escape?*

A *list* poem is another form of poetry you might write. Remember the song "My Favorite Things" from the movie *The Sound of Music*? This song is a kind of list poem which lists and rhymes things coming under the category of favorite things. Such a poem can be a list of many different things, or it can be kept to one category such as your favorite desserts, games, or times. An example follows.

> Graham crackers,
> Peanut butter,
> Hot fresh bread—
> These are the best, I've always said.
> But if you have to choose to eat
> Something else instead,
> Ask for cherries, apples—fresh and ripe and sweet.

Write a list poem about your favorite things, or write one about winter, a month, summer vacation, things in nature, or any topic you wish. Try to make it rhyme.

There are many other kinds of poems, of course. Use one of these forms or invent your own form. Poetry allows you to be your best self.

Writer's Guide *(cont.)*

❏ *Short Stories*

A short story is just what its name suggests—a story which is short. To write a short story for your class magazine, follow these rules:

- Write three handwritten pages or less.
- Choose a likeable main character.
- Give your character a problem to solve.
- Put something in the character's way, something which tries to prevent a solution for the problem.
- Help your character solve his problem.

If you think about it, you might even be able to come up with a surprise ending. Whatever you do, don't give away your ending until the very last paragraph! And remember to use lots of specific nouns and verbs but not too many adjectives and adverbs. You can paint the best word pictures with nouns and verbs.

❏ *My Favorite Animal*

Write a one-page story about an animal in your life—your pet or someone else's animal, maybe even an animal you saw at the zoo, the circus, or on a television show. Tell about the crazy things your animal does and why you like it so much. Include a photograph or hand-drawn picture of your animal.

To make your story even more fun, try typing it in the shape of your animal. (**Hint:** Draw a large pencil outline of the animal on a blank piece of paper first. Then type your story inside the outline, trying to get the typed lines to begin and end as close to the drawing lines as you can. Finally, erase your drawing lines.)

❏ *Movie, Television, Music, or Book Review*

Write about a movie or television program you have seen, music you have heard, or a book you have read. Describe your subject and tell why you like or do not like it. When writing a review, remember the following rules:

1. Do not give away the ending of a book, movie, or television program.
2. Do give the title and where and when it can be seen or read.
3. Do give good reasons for why you do or do not like it.
4. Name some good and (if appropriate) bad things about it.
   - Do the characters seem real?
   - Does it make you feel good, or does it scare you?
   - Do you recommend it to your friends?
   - Does it remind you of other stories, programs, or music?

Writer's Guide *(cont.)*

❏ *The Most Interesting Person I've Ever Met*

All of us know interesting people. Yours may be a grandfather or parent, a neighbor or teacher, a friend, or even someone you've never actually met but only seen. Write about this person in your life. What is the story of this person's life? How do you know the person? What effect on you has this person had? Has this person ever told you a story about him or herself which shows the person's personality? Tell it again so your reader can see and understand the person the way you do.

Interview the person if you can. Ask questions such as these:

> *"What was your childhood like?"*
> *"What was your schooling like?"* (Ask the first two questions if the person is an adult.)
> *"Have you always lived here?"*
> *"What was the place you came from like?"*
> *"What is the most important thing for me to tell people about you?"*

After you have gathered all your information about the person, put the things you have learned into some kind of order. Some people like to outline before they write, and you may want to do this. Close with telling something about the person which best shows the person's personality.

❏ *Editorials and Letters to the Editor*

Most magazines, like newspapers, have editorials written by the editor of the magazine or by the editor's staff members. Many magazines include a letters-to-the-editor section as well. Editorials and letters to the editor contain both facts and opinions.

An editorial usually speaks of something many people feel strongly about. It might be about neighborhood gangs, graffiti, animal abuse, overpopulation, cheating, traffic safety, or family conflict. In an editorial, the editor writes an introduction which takes a stand about the topic. An editorial about Halloween might begin like this one.

> *Each year when Halloween comes near, small groups of people begin complaining about how the holiday makes witches and goblins seem jolly and innocent when they should be seen as evil. These people are being silly when they try to make Halloween into something it is not. Let's call a holiday a holiday. Halloween is simply a day of harmless fun when children can play "let's pretend."*

Another editorial on the same topic might be stated from a different point of view.

> *Each year when Halloween comes near, various groups of people point out how the holiday makes witches and goblins seem jolly and innocent when they should be seen as evil. Since the holiday actually began in pagan ceremonies marking the start of a season of cold, darkness, and decay, perhaps they have a point here that we all should consider.*

In either case this first paragraph states clearly what the rest of the editorial is going to be about. The editor will then go on to include any facts and opinions he or she has to back up what has been said in the first paragraph. The writer's purpose in writing an editorial is to persuade people that what he or she is saying is true.

Writer's Guide *(cont.)*

❏ *Editorials and Letters to the Editor* *(cont.)*

A good letter to the editor is similar to an editorial because it begins with a statement of the writer's opinion. Sometimes the letter is written in response to an article or editorial which has appeared in the magazine. A letter to the editor also tries to persuade the reader to agree with the opinion of the writer.

Write a letter to the editor telling how you feel about one of the following:

• school uniforms	• music and art in school	• new clubs
• cafeteria food	• graffiti	• needed activities
• the new math books	• computers in school	• fair rules
• school sports	• cheating	• clean school grounds

Write three paragraphs. In the first paragraph, state your opinion about the topic you have chosen. In the second paragraph, give your reasons for feeling the way you do about the subject. Include both facts and opinions. In your last paragraph, sum up what you said in the first two and draw a conclusion.

❏ *It's a Weird World*

This is a good feature to include in your magazine. Search through books like *The Guinness Book of World Records* and *Ripley's Believe It or Not* for stories of the weird and wonderful world we live in, and write about some of these strange happenings. Sometimes fact is stranger than fiction. Illustrate your story with drawings of your own.

❏ *How-To-Do-It Article*

In a how-to-do-it article, you describe the steps in completing a task. This may be harder than you think it will be, so do the following:

1. Complete the task you wish to describe to review how to do it.

2. As you complete the task, write down each step.

3. Now write about doing the task:

   • Write an introduction telling what you will explain.

   • Describe each step in simple, clear words.

   • Include a diagram or sketch, if appropriate.

   • Tell any problem a person might have completing the task.

   • Write your conclusion.

Story Starters

Cut out and distribute these story ideas to help students get started on writing their stories.

When Jordan saw the dog in the window at the pet store, he knew that was his dog. He would just have to figure out a plan to bring him home to his backyard. "Hello, Tidbit," Jordy whispered to the wiggly little puppy who was overjoyed at the attention.

Lindsay had never felt more alone in her entire life. She didn't know where her class was, she'd never seen any of these people before, and she missed her friends back home so much that she felt like something was holding onto her throat.

"My mom will be so surprised," Manuel said to himself as he got out the flour and the rice. "When she gets home, dinner will be ready to eat!" There was just one thing that he was forgetting.

Suzanne knew that the day would be one she would never forget. There was something about how the sun slanted through her bedroom window when she woke up in the morning. Even the way the air sounded was different, there was a kind of hush as if the world was holding its breath for what was to come.

"Who wants to play the lead in the school play?" Mrs. Lyle looked at the students and clutched at her clipboard. "I do," Jason said. It got really quiet and then some of the students started to laugh. "You couldn't do the lead," Kyle said, "you would have to sing and dance...AND ACT!" "I can do it," Jason said.

Tran didn't want his dad to drive him to school anymore. It wasn't because he was ashamed of his dad. His dad was just an ordinary man. It wasn't because he was ashamed of the family car. It was an ordinary car. What embarrassed him was that his whole family went with him.

Marcella hated school. It was too hard. Her teachers weren't patient with her. She didn't have very many friends. She had too much homework. And then, she met A. J., and everything changed.

Rickie wanted to be in the circus more than anything in the world. "I could be an acrobat!" "I could be a clown!" "I could be an elephant trainer!" Rickie would be glad to be anything, as long as he was in the circus, but his mom kept telling him that it was not a good idea.

Story Starters *(cont.)*

The trail led up and over a ridge. Adam didn't know where it led, but he knew he would have to keep moving.

After she heard a knock at the door, Esther opened it and found a box on the porch. The box was sky blue, and there was a pink label with her name on it.

When Joey got home from football practice, he found the house dark and empty. "Anyone here?" he called. He wandered around and was about to make himself a triple-decker peanut butter and jelly sandwich when something stopped him.

When Kellie woke up Saturday morning, she heard strange voices talking about her in the other room.

When Daniel's painting won first prize in the art contest, he was surprised and happy. His brother wasn't so happy about it, though.

When Mike and Tim got home from school, their mother said, "There will be no dinner tonight!" There were also no clean clothes, no help with homework, and no ride to soccer practice.

It was a hot and humid day, and there was no sound of birds singing. Even the dogs were too hot and lazy to bark. So when, all of the dogs in the neighborhood started to bark madly, Marco felt his skin crawl with fear and excitement.

Erin had been riding in the back seat of her family's car over many miles of flat, brown land when a billboard came into view. She sat up and stared because there was a huge picture of herself on the billboard!

In the elevator after visiting his grandpa, Jake was singing his favorite song when suddenly, the elevator stopped between floors and the lights went out.

During science class, Raul passed a note to Denny. Denny opened it and read, "Mrs. Rodriguez is an alien, look carefully at her eyes. Pass it on." Denny passed the note to Holly and then sat back to look at the teacher's eyes.

"Shhhhh...." Amy said, "What's that sound?" Cory listened intently. "What sound?" "Now THAT sound!" Amy whispered. Cory heard it that time. It was almost a wailing sound, something like a cat or a baby or a bird, but it wasn't any of those.

Story Scramble Cards

Duplicate pages 40–42 as many times as necessary so that when the cards are cut out, each student can have one from each page. Cut out the cards and place each group in a separate bag, hat, or other container. Students are to pick one card from each container.

These cards indicate the main character, the setting, and the situation to be developed for a short story or news report the students will create.

Students (individually or in groups) are then to move through the writing process by brainstorming details for each card, webbing, drafting, using peer response sheets, editing, revising, and publishing the work.

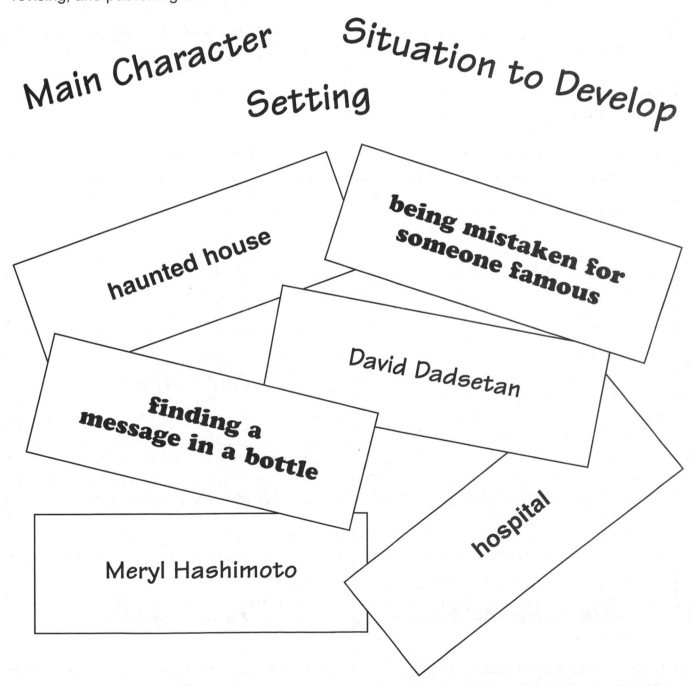

Main Character   Situation to Develop   Setting

being mistaken for someone famous

haunted house

David Dadsetan

finding a message in a bottle

hospital

Meryl Hashimoto

Story Scramble Cards *(cont.)*

Main Character

Chase Fleming	Felipe Arca
Frazier Cunningham	Meryl Hashimoto
Alex Martin	Deancy Okoebor
Briana Turkel	Jason Grimm
Kristina Lorioux	Paul Miriani
Michoe Whitney	Nicole McMaster
David Dadsetan	A. J. Logan

Story Scramble Cards *(cont.)*

Setting

amusement park	train station
cruise ship	spaceship
school	zoo
dude ranch	haunted house
costume party	TV station
hospital	bowling alley
mountain	circus

Story Scramble Cards *(cont.)*

Situation to Develop

traveling through time	speaking every language
discovering a long-lost identical twin	talking to animals
being mistaken for someone famous	being able to live under the sea
discovering the fountain of youth	being trapped
shrinking to the size of a mouse	finding a message in a bottle
getting into my computer program	finding a bag full of money
predicting the future	finding an alien

Metaphors

Metaphors compare two different things without using *like* or *as*. (**Example:** His feet are giant boulders.) Use comparison words to complete the metaphors.

1. The clown is a _____

2. The bird is a _____

3. The elephant is a _____

4. The falcon is a _____

5. The moon was _____

6. The snow was _____

7. The baby was _____

8. The game was _____

9. The thunder and lightning were _____

10. The field was _____

11. The sand is _____

12. The river is _____

13. The grandparents were _____

14. The dress is _____

15. That hat is _____

I Feel As Silly As...

A good way to warm up creative muscles is to play with similes. A simile compares two different things.

Examples

"I feel as angry as a hornet's nest!"
"I feel as tired as a rag doll that's lost its stuffing."

Now you try some. Be as creative as you can.

I feel as limp as a(n) _____

I feel as happy as a(n) _____

I feel as strong as a(n) _____

I feel as silly as a(n) _____

I feel as sad as a(n) _____

I feel as angry as a(n) _____

I feel as excited as a(n) _____

I feel as frightened as a(n) _____

I feel as light as a(n) _____

I feel as grumpy as a(n) _____

I feel as slow as a(n) _____

I feel as hungry as a(n) _____

I feel as sleepy as a(n) _____

Extension: After reading a book or story, write some character descriptions using similes. For instance, you might draw a character at the top of the page and then describe the character. Here is an example: "She was as skinny as the painted line dividing the highway. Her hair was as mossy and clumped as seaweed. Her eyes were as brown as chocolate. She was as feisty as a bunch of seagulls fighting over an open bag of potato chips."

Letter Form

Below is a letter to the editor using the standard form for writing a business letter. This is the form you would use when writing a letter to the editor of a magazine.

- Centered at the top of the page, put your name, address, and telephone number.
- On the left side of the first page put the date, name, title, and address of the editor to whom you are writing.
- Two lines below the name and address of the person to whom you are writing, begin your letter with *Dear Mr.*, *Dear Mrs.*, *Dear Ms.*, or *Dear Editor.*
- Keep your writing clear and easy to read. Remember—write for your reader!
- Sign your name at the end of the letter under the closing word *Sincerely.*

Betty Jane Smith
8888 Jenny Dr.
San Jose, CA 95523
(415) 222-3333

January 4, 1997

Mr. Darrell E. Whitcomb, Editor
Young Times Magazine
4422 Williams Way
Carrolltown, VA 22110

Dear Mr. Whitcomb,

I have noticed that people are using words incorrectly, and I would like to see you do something about it.

One of the things they do is use the word "myself" when they should be using "I" instead. Yesterday I heard a man on television saying, "Myself and a friend went to the football game together." I asked my mother if this was right, and she said he should have said, "A friend and I went to the football game."

I think it's wrong for people who are on television to speak English incorrectly. Young children just learning how to talk might learn to speak incorrectly from hearing it that way on television. Do you think you could have an article in the magazine telling us how to speak correctly?

I read your magazine every week and like it very much.

Sincerely,

Betty Jane Smith

Writing a Letter

On the following form, write a letter to the editor about something which concerns you.

_____

_____

_____

_____

_____

_____

_____

_____

_____

_____

_____

_____

_____

_____

_____

_____

_____

_____

_____

_____

Pen Pal Pointers

When you get the mail, what things would you want to open first? The envelope that says, "You may have already won...," the one that has pictures of detergent boxes on the outside, the one that says, "You can help save the cockroach"? Or do you open the personal, handwritten letter first? There is no mail like a personal letter. That's what we like to open first! Delight your friends and relatives by sending them personal letters. Here are some of the ways you can send creative, personal mail.

- Send a photograph as a postcard. Glue your photo to a piece of cardboard cut to the same size as the photograph, and add your message, the address, and a postcard stamp.

- Write a letter on heavy paper and then cut it into pieces like a jigsaw puzzle. Send the pieces in an envelope and let the recipient put it together before he or she can read it.

- Use butcher paper to create a mural or poster letter, complete with big, colorful drawings or paintings. Roll up your letter and mail it in a mailing tube (available at post offices or office supply stores).

- Press flowers and when they are dry and flat, glue them to the top of a piece of letter stationery or the front of a blank card. Write your letter and mail it.

- Use a scanner or a color copier to create unique stationary full of photos of you and your friends. Write with boldly colored inks.

- Make stationery using colorful paper and hole punches. Punch patterns in one sheet of paper and layer it over another color.

- Make a distant cousin or aunt/uncle your pen pal. Find out everything you can about him or her. Exchange photographs and swap stories.

- Watercolor some sheets of paper in pastels. When dry, write letters over the surface of the paintings.

When you send a letter to a distant friend or relative, enclose things like interesting newspaper clippings and photos from your local paper, programs or awards, small souvenirs (a curl from your baby brother's head—with your mom's permission), a feather from a local bird, a small shell or rock, a button, bumper sticker, one of your school papers (with a good grade, of course), a bit of fabric, etc.

Remember to include details in your letters. Don't just write, "Dad was mad." Write, "You should have seen his face, it crumpled up like a tight fist and turned as red as mom's lipstick." Include plenty of details about your life: the girl you have a crush on and what she is like, the embarrassing thing that happened to you recently, what things have made you mad, sad, or glad.

Also, always comment on what was written to you in your pen pal's last letter, and ask questions so your pen pal will have things to tell you next time.

Always be kind and courteous in your letters to others.

Journal Writing

Writing in your journal can have many benefits. In addition to practicing writing, journal writing can help you make sense of things, sort out your feelings, find new ways to express yourself, and give you confidence. It's a good idea to write in your journal every day. A journal can be like a friend—someone to confide in. Use the space below to practice journal writing.

Journal Starts

Can't think of what to write about in your journal today? Maybe one of these ideas will get you started.

The best thing that happened to me yesterday was...	I can't wait to drive...
When I grow up, I want to...	I would like a new pet...
Last week I had a bad day when everything went wrong...	What I would like to change about myself is...
In five years, I will be...	I really like...
If I were to write a book, it would be about...	The ugliest thing I ever saw...
I would like to change the rules at my house...	My favorite memory is...
If I could sail around the world...	I wish I could...
The one thing I would like to change about the world is...	After school I like to...

Vocabulary Concentration

Cut out the cards on this page and the next one and turn them facedown. Turn over two, and if the definition matches the word, take the pair. You may use a dictionary if you need to. If the cards do not match, turn them back over and try again. You may play by yourself or with a partner.

Vocabulary Words

entice	barrack	edible
gondola	molt	outcast
bamboozle	catastrophe	headquarters
decline	bacteria	prohibit

© Teacher Created Materials, Inc.

Vocabulary Concentration *(cont.)*

Definitions

to attract or tempt	building for lodging soldiers	able to be eaten
water taxi	to shed skin	one rejected by society
trick or cheat	major disaster	center of operations
refuse	one-celled germ	forbid

Spelling Quest

Use a dictionary to help you answer the questions on this quest.

1. Find a word that uses the spelling rule "*i* before *e*."

2. Find a word that breaks the spelling rule "*i* before *e*."

3. Find a word that follows the spelling rule "When two vowels go walking, the first does the talking."

4. Find a word that breaks the rule in problem number three.

5. Find a word in which you have to change the *y* to *i* before adding an ending.

6. Find a word where you keep the letter *y* when an ending is added.

7. Find a word that is always capitalized.

8. Find two words that sound alike but are spelled differently.

9. Find two words that are spelled the same but are pronounced differently.

10. Find a word with four syllables.

Center Dictionary

When you come across an unfamiliar word, look it up. Then, fill in this form and place it in the center's dictionary file. Your teacher will laminate your page and add it to the dictionary created by you and your classmates. If you wish, you may add an illustration in the right hand box.

word:	
definition:	
word:	
definition:	

Punctuation Concentration

Directions: Copy the sentence cards (pages 54 and 55) on colored cardstock and two sets of the punctuation cards (page 56) on a different colored cardstock. If colored paper is not available, simply mark the backs of one set of cards to distinguish them from the other set. Cut the sentence cards apart, shuffle them, and place them facedown. Do the same with the punctuation cards.

How to Play: The first player turns over a sentence card, reads it, and decides what punctuation mark(s) is missing. He or she then chooses a punctuation card. If it is a needed card (i.e., the punctation mark shown is required for the player's sentence card to be correct), the player keeps the pair and takes another turn. If it is not a match, the player returns both cards facedown to their original positions, and the next player takes a turn. The game continues until there are no sentence cards left. The player with the most cards wins.

Sentence Cards

Do you want some ice cream	Yes I want to go
The house is on fire	We went to Paris France
My dogs name is Chubba	What is your favorite movie

Punctuation Concentration *(cont.)*

Sentence Cards *(cont.)*

I'm hungry said Fred	School starts at 8 15
She was cold she put on a jacket	It is Joes cat
Help	Sue said I like chocolate cake
They went to sleep at 10 30	Maria had to have an x ray taken.

Punctuation Concentration *(cont.)*

Punctuation Cards

＿ ＿ ＿ ＿ ＿ **?** question mark	＿ ＿ ＿ ＿ ＿**,** comma
＿ ＿ ＿ ＿ ＿ **!** exclamation point	＿ ＿ ＿ ＿ ＿ **.** period
" ＿ ＿ ＿ ＿ ＿ opening quotation mark	**"** ＿ ＿ ＿ ＿ ＿ closing quotation mark
: ＿ ＿ ＿ ＿ ＿ **:** colon	**;** ＿ ＿ ＿ ＿ ＿**;** semicolon
- ＿ ＿ ＿ ＿ hyphen	**'** ＿ ＿ ＿ ＿ ＿ apostrophe

Getting Ideas

When you need to write a book report, these ideas should get you started.

Sell Your Book. Create a written or oral presentation to "sell" your book to your classmates. Include props, graphics, and visuals.

Character Pen Pal. Choose a character from your book and write a letter to him or her. Tell him or her how your life is different or similar, offer your opinions on the events of the story, say what you think of the other characters, etc.

See You in the Funny Papers. Create a comic strip about one of the scenes in the story. Include the title as well as speech and thought bubbles.

The Condensed Version. Choose five important scenes from the book. Gather six pieces of paper or cardboard, markers, pencils, tape, and whatever else you want to use. On one piece of paper or cardboard, create a cover with the book title and an illustration. On the rest of the pieces, illustrate each of the five scenes and write a summary to explain what is happening in each scene.

Put on a Jacket. Fold a brown grocery sack, or butcher paper to fit your book. With markers, paints, or pens, create a book jacket with a cover, art, and information about the book and its plot, the characters, and the author.

The Movie. What if your book was made into a movie? Create a movie poster to promote your book-turned-movie.

The Same and Different. Draw a Venn diagram and compare the similarities and differences of two of the characters. Or compare a character to yourself.

You Choose!

Think about the book you just read and answer the following questions about the book. If you need more room, use the back of this page or staple extra pages to this page.

1. Are there parts of the story that are frightening? If so, what part is the most frightening and why?

   _____

   _____

   _____

2. Is there anything in the story that is just too hard to believe? If so, what part would that be? Why is it hard to believe?

   _____

   _____

   _____

   _____

3. Who is your favorite character in the story? Why? In what ways are you like the character?

   _____

   _____

   _____

   _____

4. Is there a sad part? What is the saddest part of the story?

   _____

   _____

   _____

5. What is your favorite part of the story? Why is this part meaningful to you?

   _____

   _____

   _____

   _____

Animal or Human?

Many stories about animals or featuring animals demonstrate the abilities of some animals to do astonishing things. Sometimes they may seem almost capable of being human. In other cases, of course, they may possess characteristics that are *beyond* human abilities.

Considering the animal in the story you are reading (or have just finished reading), list 10 characteristics that are *similar* to those of humans.

1. _____
2. _____
3. _____
4. _____
5. _____
6. _____
7. _____
8. _____
9. _____
10. _____

Now list 10 characteristics that are *different* from those of humans.

1. _____
2. _____
3. _____
4. _____
5. _____
6. _____
7. _____
8. _____
9. _____
10. _____

Name one thing that humans can do that animals cannot._____

_____

The Sequel

You have finished your book, and the story has ended. Or has it? Would you like the characters to continue with their next adventure? They will in the sequel (or the continuation) of the story. Fill in this form and then on the back or another piece of paper, write an outline or synopsis (summary) of the book that would follow the one you just read.

Title of the book you read: _____

Author: _____

Title of the sequel: _____

Author (your name, of course!): _____

The characters who will appear in the sequel:_____

_____

The setting:_____

_____

The time period: _____

Will any of your characters change in a big or small way? Which characters? How will they change?

_____

_____

_____

Will there be any new characters introduced in the sequel?

_____

_____

_____

What problems will the characters be faced with in the sequel?

_____

_____

Finding Facts

Read a book that takes place in a faraway setting. Find some facts about the setting. Find facts about the local area, as well as the country and continent in which the action of your story takes place. Use encyclopedias, an atlas, other books, and the Internet, if available. List at least 10 facts about the setting of your story.

1. _____
2. _____
3. _____
4. _____
5. _____
6. _____
7. _____
8. _____
9. _____
10. _____
11. _____
12. _____
13. _____
14. _____
15. _____
16. _____
17. _____
18. _____
19. _____
20. _____

Mapping the Matter

Think about the places where the events occur in your story. In the space below, draw a map of the area and indicate where and when the important events took place. (**Note:** The events may all have taken place within a building, a small town, a large city, or even across a whole country or continent.) Make your map fit the events of your story.

Math

The Value of Art

Duplicate this page so that there is enough for two copies per student. Place the copies in the center for student use. (You may wish to cut out the pieces and place them in envelopes along copies of page 65.)

The Value of Art *(cont.)*

Use the paper coins and bills to create a design in the space below. Be as creative as you can be; the example is just to give you an idea. When you know what you want to create, glue the "money" into place. You may add color to your design. When you are finished, add up the total value of your art by computing the value of the coins and bills you used in your creation. Write the value in the space below your art.

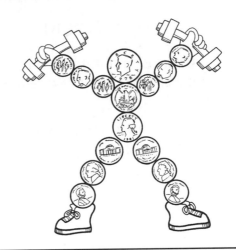

The total value is: _____

Strike It Rich!

Whose picture is on the $100,000 bill?

To discover the answer, find the difference in each problem below. Decode the name by matching the answer to its letter. Write the letter in the box below the difference.

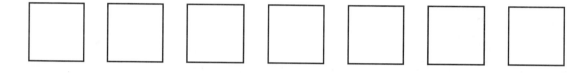

9371	3313	4530	6000	6230	3917	6792
− 4528	− 1834	− 3051	− 3781	− 1357	− 2438	− 1949

| □ | □ | □ | □ | □ | □ | □ |

7927	7203	5361	4079	7455	5386
− 3084	− 3427	− 2805	− 2834	− 5976	− 2174

| □ | □ | □ | □ | □ | □ |

1479 **O**	3776 **I**	4843 **W**	2219 **D**
4873 **R**	2556 **L**	3212 **N**	1245 **S**

Did you know?

The $100,000 bill is the highest-value bill ever printed by the United States. It was used only by government banks. The bill is no longer issued. The $100 bill is the highest value U.S. bill in circulation today.

Change For Fifty Cents

There are over 75 ways to make change for 50 cents. Work with a friend to list as many ways as you can. List the coins in order on each line, from largest to smallest. (**Hint:** Working from large to small coins will also help you find more ways to make change.) The list has been started for you. If you need more space, continue your list on the back of this paper.

Use the following abbreviations:

hd (half dollar)   **q** (quarter)   **d** (dime)   **n** (nickel)   **p** (penny)

1. _____ 1 hd _____

2. _____ 2 q _____

3. _____

4. _____

5. _____

6. _____

7. _____

8. _____

9. _____

10. _____

11. _____

12. _____

13. _____

14. _____

15. _____

The Value of Words

In the value box, each letter of the alphabet has been given a dollar value. To find the value of a word, add the values of all the letters. For example, the word "school" would be worth $72 (19 + 3 + 8 + 15 + 15 + 12 = 72). Write words with appropriate values in each of the boxes below.

$10 Words	$20 Words

$50 Words	$100 Words

$101–$150 Words	$151–$200 Words

VALUE BOX		
A	=	$1
B	=	$2
C	=	$3
D	=	$4
E	=	$5
F	=	$6
G	=	$7
H	=	$8
I	=	$9
J	=	$10
K	=	$11
L	=	$12
M	=	$13
N	=	$14
O	=	$15
P	=	$16
Q	=	$17
R	=	$18
S	=	$19
T	=	$20
U	=	$21
V	=	$22
W	=	$23
X	=	$24
Y	=	$25
Z	=	$26

Solve These If You Can!

Can you find the answers to these word problems? When you are finished, use the blank form on page 70 to write some of your own word problems.

1. Paul went horseback riding. He paid 2 five-dollar bills and 3 quarters. He received one dollar bill and a dime in change. How much did it cost Paul to go riding?

   _____

   _____

2. Amy gave the fast food clerk 3 one-dollar bills, a quarter, 2 dimes, and 3 pennies. The clerk told her she still owes a nickel. How much was Amy's lunch?

   _____

   _____

3. When Lan went bowling, he gave the clerk 2 one-dollar bills, a half dollar and a quarter. The clerk gave him 2 dimes in change. How much did it cost Lan to bowl?

   _____

   _____

4. Kimi wanted to buy a cake mix. She looked in her wallet and counted 2 one-dollar bills and 3 nickels. She would need a half-dollar more. How much was the cake mix?

   _____

   _____

5. Alvaro bought a ticket to a concert.   He paid with a ten-dollar bill and a five-dollar bill. He received 2 one-dollar bills in change. How much was the concert ticket?

   _____

   _____

6. Sheila wanted to buy a new swimsuit. She had 2 ten-dollar bills, but would need a five-dollar bill and 2 one-dollar bills. How much would the new swimsuit cost?

   _____

   _____

Solve My Problems, If You Can!

Here are some word problems created by: _____

Cookie Math

The following word problems are based on some interesting statistics about chocolate chip cookies.

> **Fact A:** *Seven billion chocolate chip cookies are consumed annually in the United States.*

Exercises

1. Write seven billion in numerals. _____

2. In order to find out how many cookies are consumed on average by every person in the United States, what other information would you need to know in order to solve the problem? _____

3. Where could you find that information? _____

4. How would you solve the problem? _____

> **Fact B:** *Ninety million bags of chocolate morsels are sold each year, enough to make 150 million pounds (68 million kg) of cookies.*

Exercises

1. Write a ratio to show the number of bags of chocolate morsels to the number of pounds of cookies. _____

   Reduce it to its lowest terms. _____

2. How many pounds of cookies can be made from 30 million bags of chocolate morsels? How could this problem be solved? _____

> **Fact C:** *The 150 million pounds (68 million kg) of cookies in Fact B above is enough to circle the globe 10 times.*

Exercises

1. How many cookies does it take to circle the globe once? _____

2. How many cookies would it take to circle the globe 15 times? _____

> **Fact D:** *Although the original Toll House burned to the ground in 1984, it was still baking cookies in an annex until the new one was rebuilt. Some thirty-three thousand cookies a day were baked there.*

Exercises

1. If 33,000 cookies were baked there each day, how many cookies would be baked in a week? _____

2. If baking goes on 24 hours a day, how many cookies, on the average, are baked each hour? _____

Metric System

Measure the following items found in the center or on your own body, using metric tools, and record your findings. You may use the ruler on this page to help you start measuring.

1. the width of your shoe

   _____

2. the length of the pen or pencil you are using

   _____

3. the length of a paper clip

   _____

4. the width of the same paper clip

   _____

5. the length of your shoe

   _____

6. the length of your arm from the wrist to the elbow

   _____

7. the width of this piece of paper

   _____

8. the width of your hand

   _____

9. the length of your thumb

   _____

10. the width of your thumb

   _____

Customary System

Measure the following items found in the center or on your body, using U.S. Customary system (inches) tools and record your findings. You may use the ruler on this page to help you start measuring.

1. the width of your shoe

   _____

2. the length of the pen or pencil you are using

   _____

3. the length of a paper clip

   _____

4. the width of the same paper clip

   _____

5. the length of your shoe

   _____

6. the length of your arm from the wrist to the elbow

   _____

7. the width of this piece of paper

   _____

8. the width of your hand

   _____

9. the length of your thumb

   _____

10. the width of your thumb

    _____

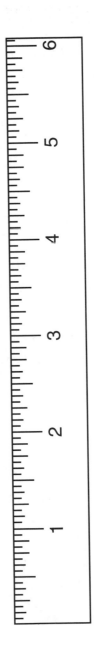

New System

Create your own measurement system. Choose an item, such as a favorite pencil, eraser, or book. Measure the items below and record your findings (for example: 4½ erasers, three pencils, or ¼ of a book width.)

1. the width of your shoe _____

2. the length of a pen or pencil you are using _____

3. the length of a paper clip _____

4. the width of the same paper clip _____

5. the length of your shoe_____

6. the length of your arm from the wrist to the elbow_____

7. the width of this piece of paper _____

8. the width of your hand _____

9. the width of your desk _____

10. the width of your thumb _____

Comparing Systems

Here is an example of a conversion chart for comparing metric measurements to the U.S. customary system.

| One inch = 2.54 cm | One foot = 30 cm | One yard = 91 cm |

In the space below, compare your own measuring system to the U.S. customary system and the metric system.

New System Conversion Table

Object	New System	Metric System	Customary System
The width of your shoe			
The length of the pen or pencil			
The length of a paper clip			
The width of the same paper clip			
The length of your shoe			
The length of your arm from the wrist to the elbow			
The width of this piece of paper			
The width of your hand			
The length of your thumb			
The width of your thumb			

Measuring Without a Ruler

Each of these items can be used as a measurement tool by multiplying its length by the number of times it is used to measure.

- Your arms stretched out from fingertip to fingertip

- Your feet (place one foot in front of the other to measure)

- A belt

- A tie

- A hair ribbon

- A shoelace

- A pencil

These items can also be used.

- A standard sheet of paper is 8.5" x 11" (21 cm x 28 cm)

- Floor tiles are often 12" x 12" (30 cm x 30 cm)

- The average piece of sandwich bread is about 4" x 4" (10 cm x 10 cm)

- A penny is approximately ¾" (2 cm) wide.

- A quarter is approximately 1" (2.54 cm) wide.

- A U.S. paper bill is a little over 6" (15 cm) long, and almost 3" (8 cm) wide.

Measurement Challenge

How quickly can you find the measurements below? Work alone, and time yourself for each page using a stopwatch or watch. Write your time at the bottom of each page. Or, if your teacher gives you the okay, race a partner. You may also work with a partner to come up with the answers, if you prefer.

Task Cards

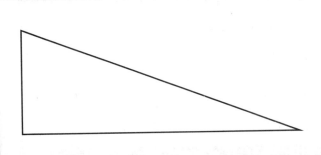

1. Rectangle

- Length = 13 feet

- Perimeter = 42 feet

- Width = _____feet

2. Triangle

- Side 1 = 29 centimeters

- Side 2 = 23 centimeters

- Perimeter = 86 centimeters

- Side 3 = _____centimeters

3. Square

- Length of each side = 31 centimeters

- Area = _____square centimeters

4. Rectangle

- Length = 18 meters

- Area = 162 meters squared

- Width = _____meters

Measurement Challenge *(cont.)*

Task Cards

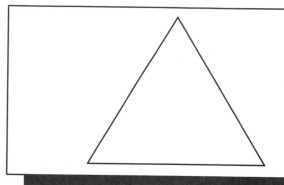

5. Triangle

- Side 1 = 18 inches
- Sides 2 and 3 are equal.
- Perimeter = 42 inches
- Side 2 = _____ inches
- Side 3 = _____ inches

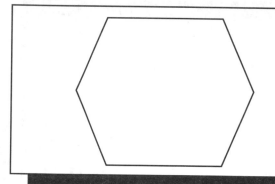

6. Hexagon

- All sides are 17 feet.
- Perimeter = _____ feet

7. Square

- Area = 49 square meters
- Length of each side = _____ meters

8. Rectangle

- Width = 9 feet
- Length = 18 feet
- Area = _____ square feet

Drawing to Scale

1. Use graph paper with ¹/₄" (.64 cm) squares. Make a few measurements before you decide on an appropriate scale to use. You can tape sheets of graph paper together if necessary.

2. Pick out a large building or feature on your school's campus to measure and use as a guide for estimating the size of the other buildings or rooms. (Get an idea of size by "pacing off" the length or width of something. Measure your stride and then count the number of steps you take. This is not exact, but it will help.)

3. Make a rough sketch in the space below. Then make some more exact measurements before you try to draw a final plan on the graph paper.

Prime Time

Mathematicians put numbers into two categories—*prime* or *composite*. A *prime number* is a number with only two factors: one and itself. A *composite number* has more than two factors.

A Greek mathematician named Eratosthenes invented a method to see if a number is prime or composite; that method is called the *Sieve of Eratosthenes*. He arranged the numbers from 1 to 100 and used divisibility rules to find the prime numbers. Use the numbers in the box below and follow the steps to find the prime numbers.

- The number 1 is a special case. It is neither prime nor composite. Put a box around number 1.
- Number 2 is a prime number, so circle 2. Cross out all the numbers divisible by 2.
- Number 3 is a prime number, so circle 3. Then cross out all numbers divisible by 3.
- The next uncrossed number is 5. Circle 5 and then cross off all the multiples of 5.
- Circle 7. 7 is a prime number. Cross off all the multiples of 7.
- Any numbers that are left are prime, so circle them.

1	2	3	4	5	6	7	8	9	10
11	12	13	14	15	16	17	18	19	20
21	22	23	24	25	26	27	28	29	30
31	32	33	34	35	36	37	38	39	40
41	42	43	44	45	46	47	48	49	50
51	52	53	54	55	56	57	58	59	60
61	62	63	64	65	66	67	68	69	70
71	72	73	74	75	76	77	78	79	80
81	82	83	84	85	86	87	88	89	90
91	92	93	94	95	96	97	98	99	100

Tangrams

Reproduce the tangram pattern on page 82 on various colored sheets of construction paper. Make plenty of extra copies so that students will be able to manipulate them and also create art (with the pieces glued into place). Challenge students to create animal shapes similar to those below using only the shapes from one pattern. Have them also try other shapes such as houses, cars, or letters of the alphabet. After they have had time to manipulate the pieces to form new shapes, have students create original art by having them plan and glue colorful shapes on paper. They may use more than one tangram pattern for their creations.

Tangrams *(cont.)*

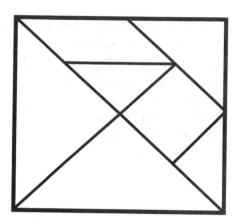

**small tangram
puzzle pattern**

large tangram puzzle pattern

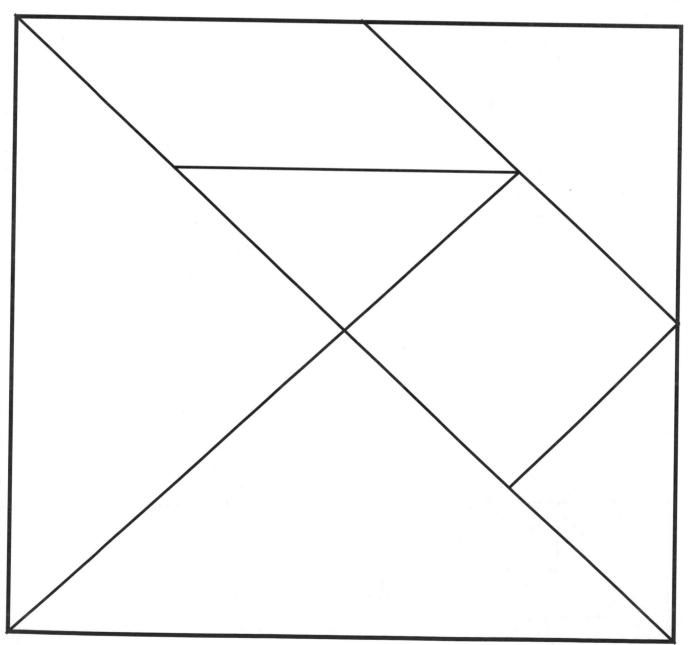

Tangrams *(cont.)*

Using the tangram shapes and a ruler, draw one or two pictures in the space below. (You may create a pleasing pattern or the shape of an animal, person, tree, etc.) Place your drawings in the tangrams file so other students can arrange tangram shapes to try to make the shapes you have drawn.

Symmetry

Using the squares as a guide, draw the other half of the figure and then color the picture.

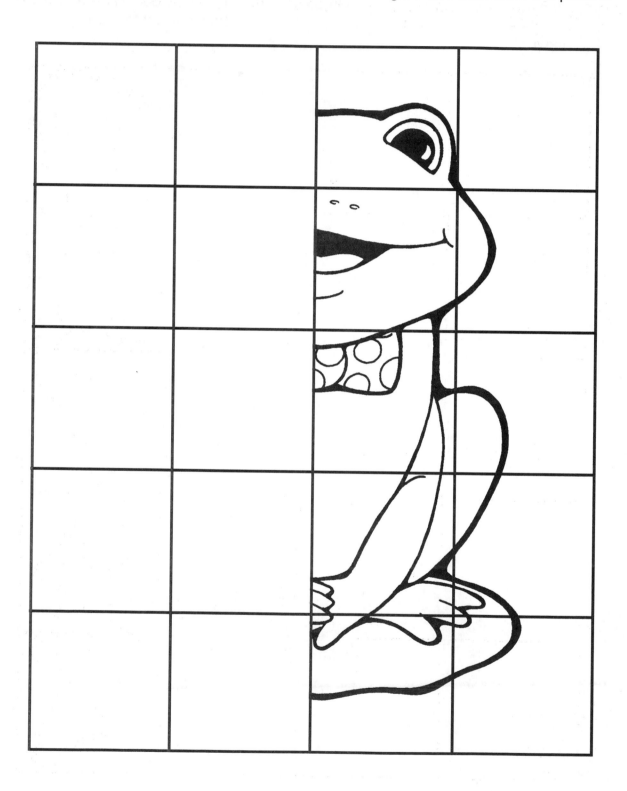

More Symmetry

Using the squares as a guide, draw the other half of the figure and then color the picture.

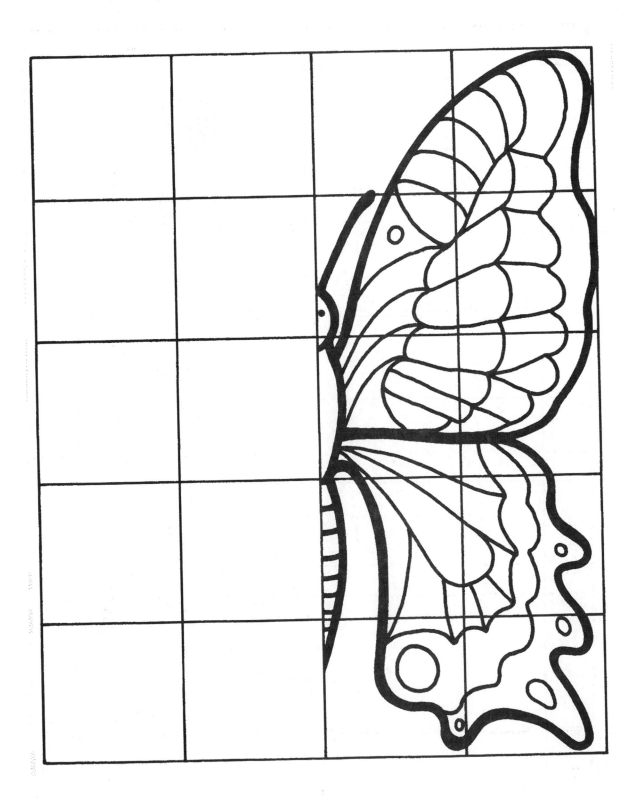

Addition and Subtraction

Place + and – signs between the digits so that both sides of each equation are equal.

1.	6 4 1 2 6 2 = 15
2.	9 1 3 1 4 1 = 5
3.	9 3 4 1 2 3 = 14
4.	5 1 1 3 4 6 = 6
5.	9 8 6 3 5 3 = 8
6.	2 1 8 9 3 5 = 20
7.	5 3 2 4 1 5 = 12
8.	4 9 3 7 3 1 = 11
9.	7 6 2 8 7 1 = 3
10.	9 9 9 2 2 8 = 1

Addition and Subtraction *(cont.)*

Place + and − signs between the digits so that both sides of each equation are equal.

1.	9	8	6	3	5	1	=	6
2.	5	3	4	4	2	9	=	17
3.	5	3	2	4	1	5	=	2
4.	3	2	1	4	1	3	=	6
5.	5	1	1	3	4	8	=	18
6.	4	9	3	7	3	1	=	19
7.	2	1	8	9	3	5	=	20
8.	8	7	1	4	4	6	=	14
9.	7	6	2	9	9	3	=	0
10.	3	5	3	9	6	5	=	15

Multiplication and Division

Place x and ÷ signs between the digits so that both sides of each equation are equal.

1.	75	3	4	2	100	250	=	20
2.	15	6	9	3	4	10	=	12
3.	6	8	12	3	6	9	=	8
4.	144	12	3	6	5	10	=	3
5.	14	64	8	8	4	4	=	14
6.	32	8	1	10	3	10	=	12
7.	44	11	7	2	7	11	=	88
8.	81	3	9	3	7	21	=	3
9.	18	9	4	7	4	2	=	7
10.	100	10	3	5	3	15	=	30

Multiplication and Division *(cont.)*

Place x and ÷ signs between the digits so that both sides of each equation are equal.

1.	81	9	7	21	6	2	=	9
2.	12	6	2	12	4	5	=	15
3.	88	11	3	4	12	8	=	9
4.	108	4	9	5	6	30	=	3
5.	54	9	6	2	8	15	=	135
6.	32	2	8	12	3	2	=	16
7.	15	5	7	3	7	5	=	45
8.	91	13	3	5	4	21	=	20
9.	33	11	5	2	6	21	=	105
10.	100	100	12	2	3	9	=	8

Calculator Fun

Do each math problem on your calculator. Then, turn the calculator upside-down to find an answer for each of the following clues.

	Number	**Word**
1. 1,000 − 229 = not feeling well	_____	_____
2. 5,285 + 1,251 + 1,199 = the opposite of buy	_____	_____
3. 70,000 − 34,999 = not secured	_____	_____
4. 314 + 215 + 181 = petroleum	_____	_____
5. 0.5731 + 0.2003 = hola	_____	_____
6. 0.09 − 0.07 = a place for animals	_____	_____
7. 188,308 + 188,308 = to laugh in a silly way	_____	_____
8. 2,000 + 95 + 700 + 250 = foot apparel	_____	_____
9. 1,080 − 272 = Robert's nickname	_____	_____
10. 0.20202 + 0.20202 = Santa's laughter	_____	_____
11. 926 x 2 x 2 = an empty space	_____	_____
12. 3,544 + 3,011 + 550 = synonym for dirt	_____	_____
13. 801 − 163 = to ask earnestly	_____	_____
14. 101 x 5 = a call for help	_____	_____
15. .3 + .3 = the opposite of stop	_____	_____

More Calculator Fun

Answer each math problem with a calculator. When you have the answer, turn the calculator upside down to find an answer for each of the clues in parentheses. The first one is done for you.

1. (Too big) 21,000 + 14,001 = _____**35,001 (loose)**_____

2. (A sphere) 21,553 + 16,523 = _____

3. (Make honey) 10,000 − 4,662 = _____

4. (Petroleum) 142 x 5 = _____

5. (Tool for watering the garden) 7,008 ÷ 2 = _____

6. (Not feeling well) 348 + 424 − 1 = _____

7. (To cry) 0.02004 + 0.02004 = _____

8. (Boy's name) 9,376 − 1,658 = _____

9. (City in Idaho) 27,413 + 7,695 = _____

10. (Antonym for "tiny") 206 + 206 + 206 = _____

Money Maze

Find your way through the money maze. Mark the path of correct money amounts. You may
go ↑   ↔   ↗↙   or   ↖↘

$ End	7 pennies + 7 dimes = 70 cents	Start $	4 nickels + 3 dimes = 60 cents
3 pennies + 2 dimes +2 quarters = 73 cents	4 nickels + 2 dimes + 3 quarters = $1.25	5 nickels + 1 dime + 1 quarter = 55 cents	6 pennies + 6 dimes + 1 quarter = 91 cents
8 pennies + 5 dimes = 58 cents	2 pennies + 3 quarters = 76 cents	8 nickels + 3 quarters = $1.15	11 pennies + 7 dimes = 78 cents
4 quarters + 2 dimes = $1.25	2 pennies + 6 nickels + 7 dimes = $1.02	1 penny + 1 dime + 2 quarters = 61 cents	2 nickels + 3 dimes = 45 cents
8 dimes = 40 cents	17 nickels = 85 cents	7 pennies + 5 nickels = 33 cents	10 quarters = $2.50
2 pennies + 5 nickels + 3 quarters = 87 cents	11 pennies + 4 nickels = 41 cents	7 nickels + 7 dimes = $1.05	3 nickels + 1 dime + 1 quarter = 45 cents
3 pennies + 3 dimes = 35 cents	4 pennies + 7 nickels = 39 cents	3 nickels + 3 dimes + 3 quarters = $1.20	4 pennies + 3 nickels = 19 cents

Energy Facts

Learn some interesting facts about energy as you solve the problems below. Write the letters from the box in the sentence blanks, matching the letters with the corresponding answers below the blanks.

A	C	D	E	G	H
37 x 12 = ___	659 + 13 = ___	720 ÷ 16 = ___	316 – 105 = ___	67 + 39 = ___	374 ÷ 22 = ___
I	**K**	**L**	**M**	**N**	**O**
823 – 78 = ___	16 x 15 = ___	361 + 19 = ___	957 ÷ 33 = ___	500 – 135 = ___	17 x 9 = ___
R	**S**	**T**	**U**	**W**	**Y**
369 + 72 = ___	216 ÷ 8 = ___	999 – 955 = ___	62 x 4 = ___	416 + 41 = ___	488 ÷ 4 = ___

1. Anything that moves has energy of ___ ___ ___ ___ ___ ___.
    29   153   44   745   153   365

2. Energy of motion is called ___ ___ ___ ___ ___ ___ ___ energy.
    240   745   365   211   44   745   672

3. ___ ___ ___ ___ and waterfalls have kinetic energy.
    457   745   365   45

4. All light is ___ ___ ___ ___ ___ ___.
    211   365   211   441   106   122

5. ___ ___ ___ ___ is energy.
    17   211   444   44

6. ___ ___ ___ ___ ___ is energy.
    27   153   248   365   45

7. ___ ___ ___ ___ ___ ___ ___ ___ ___ ___ ___ is energy.
    211   380   211   672   44   441   745   672   745   44   122

8. One kind of energy can be ___ ___ ___ ___ ___ ___ ___ to another kind of energy.
    672   17   444   365   106   211   45

Math Trivia

1. How many minutes are in two hours? _____

2. How many dimes are in a dollar? _____

3. What is a three-sided figure called? _____

4. What does a sundial do? _____

5. Two tons is equal to how many pounds? _____

6. What mark separates the hour and the minutes when one is writing down time?

   _____

7. How many items are in a dozen? _____

8. How many sides does a hexagon have? _____

9. What do you call the result of adding two numbers? _____

10. How many centimeters are in a meter? _____

11. How many months are in half of a year? _____

12. Which plane figure has eight sides?_____

13. How many sides are there on a die? _____

14. How many years are in a decade? _____

15. How many hours are in a day? _____

More Math Trivia

1. What do we call a chart that helps compare facts and numbers or quantities?

   _____

2. Does a right angle measure 60, 90, or 180 degrees? _____

3. What do we call an area where people use the same clock time?

   _____

4. What does "C" stand for in Roman numerals? _____

5. What name is given to an eight-sided figure? _____

6. How many millimeters are in a centimeter? _____

7. How many nickels are in two dollars? _____

8. How many dots are on a die? _____

9. Will parallel lines intersect? _____

10. How much is half of 20? _____

11. How many zeros are there in the number one million? _____

12. How do we find the area of a rectangle? _____

13. Which number is a palindrome, 654 or 606? _____

14. The number 66 rounded to the nearest tens place is what number?_____

15. How many degrees are there in a circle?_____

Some More Math Trivia

1. Can a triangle have two right angles? _____

2. How many centimeters are there in three meters? _____

3. What does congruent mean? _____

   _____

4. Which weighs more, a pound of feathers or a pound of bricks?

   _____

5. What are the Roman numerals for 176? _____

6. What instrument is used to measure an angle? _____

7. In the fraction $^5/_9$, which numeral is the numerator? _____

8. How many items are in a gross? _____

9. How many sides does a decagon have? _____

10. What is $^6/_8$ reduced to its lowest terms? _____

11. How many zeros are in a billion? _____

12. Which angle is greater than 90 degrees—obtuse or acute?

   _____

13. Will perpendicular lines on the same plane ever touch? _____

14. What is the shortest distance between two points? _____

15. Is fifth an ordinal or a cardinal number? _____

Even More Math Trivia

1. How many grams are in one kilogram?

   _____

2. In Roman numerals, what letter represents 1,000?

   _____

3. What name is given to the Chinese 7-piece puzzle?

   _____

4. How many feet are in a mile?

   _____

5. Which is less, maximum or minimum?

   _____

6. What is half of 25?

   _____

7. What fraction is equivalent to 50%?

   _____

8. The world is divided into how many time zones?

   _____

9. What is the distance between the center and the edge of a circle called?

   _____

10. How many sides does a heptagon have?

    _____

11. What is 3 squared?

    _____

12. How does one calculate the square of any number?

    _____

13. Give the place value of 7 in 0.708.

    _____

14. Which angle measures less than 90 degrees, an acute or obtuse angle?

    _____

15. What kind of number is divisible by only itself and 1?

    _____

Our Personal Surveys

Use the following surveys to collect information about the class. One survey could be completed for each month of the school year, or divide the class into teams or partners to compile the information. Make copies of the graph on page 99 for students to fill in and show the results of the survey. Make an enlarged copy of each survey to post in the classroom.

1. **Birthday Survey**

   How many students have birthdays in January, February, March, and so on?

2. **Ice Cream Survey**

   How many students prefer vanilla, chocolate, strawberry, or other as their favorite ice cream flavor?

3. **Eye Color Survey**

   How many students have brown, hazel, blue, green, black, etc., eyes?

4. **Birthplace Survey**

   How many students were born locally, how many in other places, how many outside of the country, etc.?

5. **Seasons Survey**

   How many students prefer winter, spring, summer, or autumn?

6. **Subjects Survey**

   How many students prefer spelling, math, social studies, art, etc., as their favorite subject?

7. **Hair Color Survey**

   How many students have black, brown, red, blonde, etc., hair?

8. **Pets Survey**

   How many students have dogs, cats, hamsters, fish, etc., or no pets?

9. **Transportation Survey**

   How many students walk, ride in a car, ride the bus, etc., to school?

10. **Game Survey**

   How many students prefer checkers, Monopoly®, Candyland®, etc.?

Our Personal Surveys *(cont.)*

What Is the Message?

Use the "phone code" to spell out messages for these famous persons. Check the numbers against the letters on a phone pad and figure out an appropriate word that is spelled by them. The first one has been done for you.

1. Moses 776-7438 = _____ <u>prophet</u> _____

2. Jonas Salk 822-2463 = _____

3. George Washington 765-3437 = _____

4. Helen Keller 272-4553 = _____

5. Tommy Lasorda 363-4377 = _____

6. Franklin Roosevelt 639-3325 = _____

7. Amelia Earhart 284-2867 = _____

8. Milton Hershey 437-7439 = _____

9. Kristi Yamaguchi 752-8464 = _____

10. George Washington Carver 732-6887 = _____

11. Judy Blume and Beverly Cleary 288-4677 = _____

12. Jack the Ripper 845-5246 = _____

13. Fred Astaire 326-2464 = _____

14. Ted Kennedy 736-2867 = _____

15. Marie Curie 243-6478 = _____

Scrambled Math

Can you unscramble the following words to find the math terms?   Write the correct word on the line after each scrambled word.

1. dad _____

2. mus _____

3. roze _____

4. lahf _____

5. slup _____

6. sinum _____

7. nitodida _____

8. geanevit _____

9. gidit _____

10. citsaamthem _____

11. trasucbt _____

12. simet _____

13. viddie _____

14. tracifon _____

15. bumner _____

Math True or False

Before each of the following statements, circle **T** if the statement is true or **F** if the statement is false. On the lines below, explain any "false" responses.

1. T F   Three is an even number.

2. T F   A hexagon has fewer sides than an octagon.

3. T F   In Roman numerals, IX is 11.

4. T F   A triangle has four sides.

5. T F   All prime numbers are odd numbers.

6. T F   A rectangle has four even sides.

7. T F   Numismatics is the science of numbers.

8. T F   Only four months of the year have thirty days.

9. T F   Pi is 3.41.

10. T F   Anything multiplied by zero equals zero.

_____

_____

_____

_____

_____

_____

_____

_____

_____

_____

_____

How Many?

1. . . . sides in a dodecagon?

_____

2. . . . items in a baker's dozen?

_____

3. . . . rings on the Olympic flag?

_____

4. . . . years in a century?

_____

5. . . . original colonies in the United States?

_____

6. . . . sides does a pentagon have?

_____

7. . . . wheels on a unicycle?

_____

8. . . . hours in a week?

_____

9. . . . days in a leap year?

_____

10. . . . years in a millennium?

_____

11. . . . cards in a standard deck?

_____

12. . . . centimeters in a meter?

_____

13. . . . degrees in a right angle?

_____

14. . . . planets in our solar system?

_____

15. . . . eyes on the Cyclops?

_____

16. . . . keys on a piano?

_____

17. . . . bones in a human body?

_____

18. . . . degrees in a circle?

_____

19. . . . events are in a decathlon?

_____

20. . . . squares on a checkerboard?

_____

Science

Science Experiments Form

This form can be used with any classroom experiment.

Name _____ Date _____

Title of Experiment _____

| **Question** | **What do I want to find out?** |

_____

_____

| **Hypothesis** | **What do I think I will find out?** |

_____

_____

| **Procedure** | **How will I find out? (List step-by-step)** |

1. _____

_____

2. _____

_____

3. _____

_____

4. _____

_____

5. _____

_____

| **Results** | **What actually happened?** |

_____

_____

| **Conclusions** | **What did I learn?** |

_____

The Sensational Submarine

Question: Why does an eyedropper rise and fall in a bottle of water?

Materials

- eyedropper
- empty 2-liter plastic soda bottle
- drinking glass
- water
- data-capture sheet (page 108)

Procedure

(You may wish to demonstrate this activity first. Then allow students to try the experiment and complete the data-capture sheet at a center.)

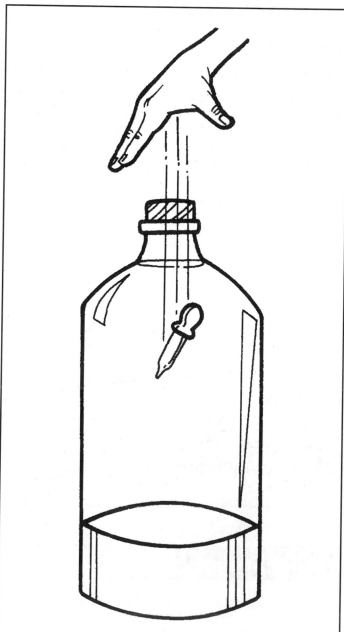

1. Fill the soda bottle with water almost to the top. Fill the drinking glass with water.

2. Remove the rubber bulb from the eyedropper and place the dropper into the drinking glass of water. When the eyedropper (submarine) becomes full of water, place the rubber bulb back on but do not remove the eyedropper from the glass during this process. Remove the eyedropper from the glass and gently squeeze out enough water so that the dropper is two-thirds full.

3. Place the eyedropper in the bottle and screw on the cap tightly. (If the eyedropper goes to the bottom of the bottle but does not come back, there is too much water in the eyedropper. Conversely, if the eyedropper remains on the surface, there is not enough water in it.)

4. Observe the setup and ask students to make suggestions about how to get the "submarine" to move up and down inside the bottle.

5. Upon completion of the "brainstorming," place both hands on either side of the soda bottle and squeeze. The eyedropper should fall to the bottom of the jug. When you release your hold, the eyedropper will climb back to the surface.

The Sensational Submarine *(cont.)*

Extensions

1. Experiment with different amounts of water in the eyedropper.

2. Experiment with different water solutions, as they will produce a variety of results. The solutions can include salt water and sugar water, as they have different densities. Also try a carbonated drink and observe the effects that carbonation and pressure have on each other.

Closure

Students review the process and then explain what method "worked" and why. Students should also make predictions about further experiments.

Conclusion

The principle illustrated here is the same as for a "real life" submarine operation. When the submarine is diving, water is carefully allowed into special tanks. In order for the sub to surface, air is forced into the same tanks to force out the water, thus making the submarine more buoyant. In the Sensational Submarine activity, by squeezing the soda bottle, the pressure inside the container increased. The water molecules were "squeezed" together and began searching for release from this pressure. Liquids do not compress as easily and quickly as gases so the air in the eyedropper was compressed together and more water entered. This added weight caused the dropper to sink. Once the pressure was released by no longer squeezing the bottle, the extra water came out of the eyedropper. The eyedropper became buoyant enough to reach the surface again.

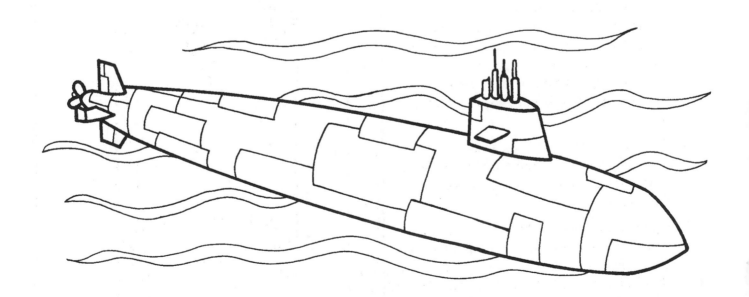

The Sensational Submarine *(cont.)*

Explain why the eyedropper rises and falls in the bottle. Write your explanation in a short paragraph.

_____

_____

_____

_____

_____

What real-life applications of this principle are there?

_____

_____

_____

_____

Draw a picture of what you observed during the demonstration as well as a real-life submarine operating on the same principle.

Observed	Realistic

Rambunctious Raisins!

Question: What causes raisins to float in soda pop?

Materials

- 5 cans of lemon-lime soda
- 1 two-liter plastic soda bottle with top cut off to provide a wide opening (label removed)
- 1 box of raisins
- stopwatch (or a watch with a second hand)
- data-capture sheet (page 110)

Procedure

(You may wish to demonstrate this activity first. Then allow students to try the experiment and complete the data-capture sheet at a center.)

1. Open the cans of lemon-lime soda and empty them into the 2-liter bottle.
2. Drop a handful of raisins into the soda. They will immediately begin to bob up and down.
3. In groups of two, students make predictions on the amount of time required for a raisin to rise and fall. Students then conduct time tests on the raisins by recording the amount of time a raisin takes to go from the bottom of the bottle to the top. The time tests should include the total amount of time for a raisin to rise and fall and reflect how long the carbonation process continues.

Extension

Students can try this on their own by scaling down the materials to one can of soda, one drinking glass, and a handful of raisins.

Closure

After observing the demonstration and completing the data capture sheets, students should be able to show their understanding of the process involved. This can be shown through discussions or a replication of the demonstration.

Conclusion

Soda pop is carbonated with carbon dioxide gas, thus producing tiny bubbles. When you add raisins to soda, the carbon dioxide molecules fix themselves to the raisins' surfaces. This "focusing" of carbon dioxide molecules results in more buoyant raisins, allowing them to rise to the surface. Once the raisins reach the top of the soda level, the carbon dioxide gas is released, and they fall to the bottom of the bottle and repeat the process again.

Rambunctious Raisins *(cont.)*

Time Tests

Test #1: Record the time it takes for raisins to travel from the bottom of the bottle to the top.

Prediction: _____ (seconds/minutes)

Conduct time tests on 10 raisins (or watch the same raisin 10 times).

Test #	Time	Test #	Time
_____	_____	_____	_____
_____	_____	_____	_____
_____	_____	_____	_____
_____	_____	_____	_____
_____	_____	_____	_____

Find the average time for the 10 tests. Show your work.

Average time: _____   Prediction: _____   Difference: _____

Test #2: Record the total time for raisins to travel from the bottom of the bottle to the top and back to the bottom again.

Prediction: _____ (seconds/minutes)

Conduct time tests on 10 raisins (or watch the same raisin 10 times).

Test #	Time	Test #	Time
_____	_____	_____	_____
_____	_____	_____	_____
_____	_____	_____	_____
_____	_____	_____	_____
_____	_____	_____	_____

Find the average time for the 10 tests. Show your works.

Average time: _____   Prediction: _____   Difference: _____

You're Full of Hot Air!

Benjamin Franklin was in Paris for the first successful hot-air balloon flight in 1883. Many people thought the invention was useless and asked, "What good is it?" Franklin's answer is the now-famous quote, "What good is a newborn baby?"

When balloons are filled with hot air, they float because they are lighter than the air around them.

Follow the directions below to make your own hot-air balloon.

Directions: Trace the pattern onto tissue paper. Enlarge the pattern first if you wish to make a larger balloon. Lift the rectangular shapes up by folding them along the dashed lines. To form the box shape of the balloon, fold the tabs in and glue to the appropriate sides. Allow glue to dry. Holding the open end of the balloon down, inflate it with the heat from a hair dryer. Watch your balloon rise!

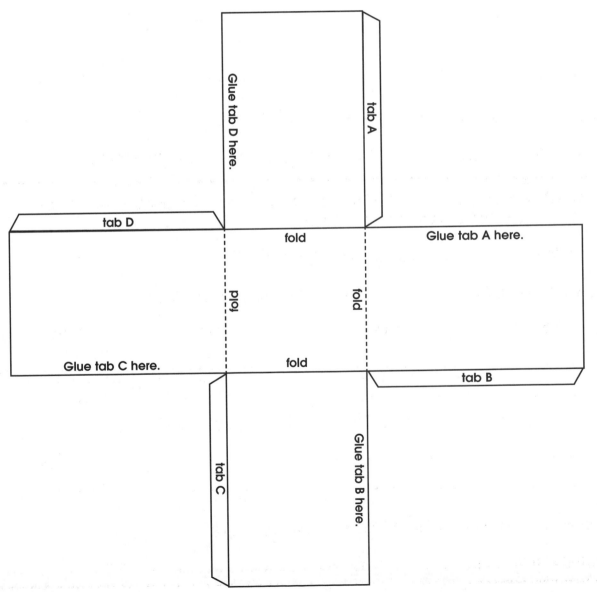

What Is Under the Sea?

Choose one of the following questions to investigate. Research in encyclopedias and books on sea life. In the space below, draw a picture to illustrate what you have learned. Write a one-page report to go with your illustration. In your report, answer the question and provide other interesting facts that are related.

- What sea animals live in the shallow areas of the ocean?
- What sea animals live near the deep areas of the ocean?
- What are the largest sea animals?

- What are the smallest sea animals?
- What sea animals are the most dangerous?
- What sea animals are used for food?
- What sea animals are endangered?

Sea Life Phyla Chart

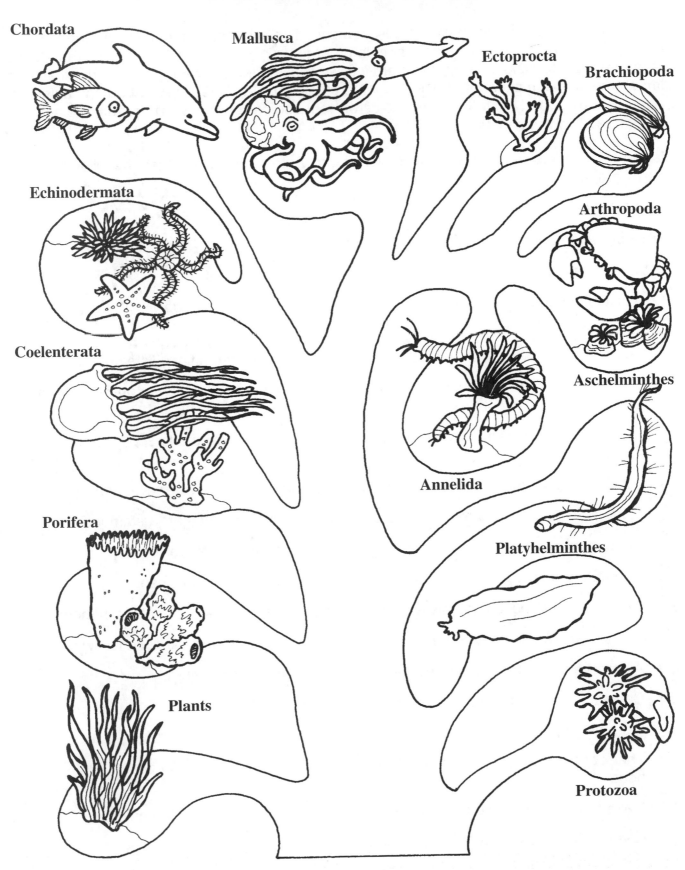

Chordata

Mallusca

Ectoprocta

Brachiopoda

Echinodermata

Arthropoda

Coelenterata

Aschelminthes

Annelida

Porifera

Platyhelminthes

Plants

Protozoa

Create a Zoo

You will be working with the mayor to design a zoo. The following instructions are for zoo design. Zookeepers must adhere to them in order to satisfy the mayor. You will need to make many sketches, to make sure that you are following instructions. When you are sure that your plan will work, use a sheet of butcher paper to create your zoo. You may cut out the animals on the next page and paste them into place on your zoo design or use the pictures to help you draw your own animals.

Mayor: "It is important to make the zoo pleasing to visitors. Please include the following in your zoo design."

- plenty of trees for shade and clean air

- a picnic area for visitors to snack or eat lunch

- fountains, ponds, or streams for the visitors and animals

- a scenic footpath that allows visitors to see every animal in the zoo

Mayor: "The animals in the zoo are very important to the community. Their health, safety, and welfare must be considered in zoo design. Please follow the instructions listed below."

- Zebras, gnus, and ostriches must have a large, sunny area in which to graze and run around.

- Giraffes must not be too close to trees; they may eat the leaves and spoil their appetites for dinner.

- Hippos, elephants, alligators, and flamingos require access to water every day.

- Rodents cannot be located near the elephants; the mice might start a stampede.

- Keep monkeys away from hyenas, or the hyenas will laugh themselves silly.

- Separate the lions, tigers, and bears because they will fight if too close.

- Rhinos need to be located away from the walls, or else they will ram holes in them.

- Be sure to place anteaters near the picnic area to keep the ant populations low.

- All monkeys, bears, and gorillas need to be far from the picnic area.

- Camels need sunny fields in which to walk about.

- Keep flamingos and ostriches far from alligators.

- The reptile building cannot be near the bird cage; a snake might escape and eat the bird eggs.

- Make the footpath close to the zebra area so that visitors may pet the animals.

- Give hyenas lots of shade under which to rest.

Create a Zoo (cont.)

Elephant	Lion	Bear	Monkey
Camel	Gorilla	Alligator	Reptiles
Rodents	Hippo	Rhino	Giraffe
Tiger	Flamingo	Ostrich	Bird Cages
Zebra	Gnu	Hyena	Anteater

Extensions

1. Draw your own zoo animals or cut pictures out of old magazines.

2. Submit a budget for food and employee wages based upon ticket prices.

3. Write a story titled "Why You Should Visit My Zoo."

Native Australian Animals

Australia Day, January 26

When the English first came to Australia in 1788, they were greeted by many unusual animals. See if you can identify the following animals. Clues and a word bank are given to help you.

WORD BANK			
koala	dingo	cuscus	wombat
emu	kangaroo	platypus	wallaby

1. __ __ __ __ __ __ u __   an egg-laying mammal with a bill and webbed feet

2. __ __ n __ __   a wild dog

3. __ __ __   nonflying bird, similar to an ostrich

4. __ __ __ __ a __ __ __   a leaping marsupial (carries its young in a pouch)

5. __ __ __ l __   tree dweller who eats only eucalyptus leaves

6. __ __ __ b __ __   resembles a bear

7. __ __ l __ __ __ __   a small kangaroo

8. __ __ __ c __ __   a tree-dwelling mammal with a long tail and tiny eyes

Animal Families and Groups

Fill in the missing information on the chart about animal families and groups.

Animal	Male	Female	Young	Group
fox	dog	_____	_____	skulk
_____	rooster	hen	_____	_____
lion	_____	lioness	_____	pride
cattle	bull	_____	calf	_____
whale	_____	cow	calf	_____
seal	bull	_____	pup	_____
ostrich	cock	hen	_____	flock
sheep	_____	ewe	_____	herd
goose	gander	_____	gosling	gaggle
kangaroo	_____	doe	_____	_____
hog	_____	sow	_____	herd
_____	billy	nanny	kid	herd

Amazing Weather Facts

Make a special spot on a bulletin board or a chart called "AMAZING!"

Print or post a new, amazing fact in this spot each day. Read and discuss this amazing weather fact each day with your class.

AMAZING!
The innuit made snow goggles 2,000 years ago!

AMAZING!
The ancient Japanese wore undershirts of bamboo to keep cool!

AMAZING!
There are 100 lightning flashes every second of every day!

AMAZING!
Droplets of water vapor in a cloud are so tiny you could fit about 15 million of them in one raindrop!

AMAZING!
Red and silver maples and poplar trees know when it's going to rain. They turn their leaves up.

AMAZING!
In England in 1881, it rained crabs and periwinkles!

AMAZING!
If we had no sun, we'd have no weather!

AMAZING!
Daytime on Venus is hot! It is 837°F!

AMAZING!
Daytime on Pluto is cold! It is −382°F!

AMAZING!
There is a building in Canada that is struck by lightning about 65 times a year!

AMAZING!
In Montreal in 1857, it rained live lizards!

AMAZING!
If a tornado travels over a lake or river, it can suck up strange things and drop them down later!

Sources: *Looking at Weather* by David Suzuki
           Weather Watch by Valerie Wyatt

Alaskan Weather

Average January Temperatures

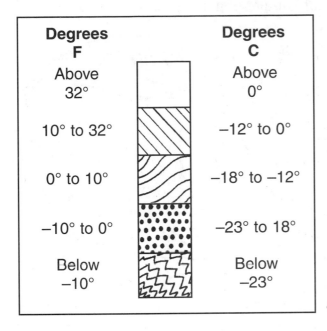

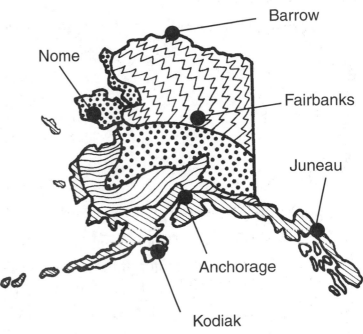

Use the map and chart above to answer the following questions:

1. What is the average January temperature of these cities?

Nome _____   Anchorage _____

Kodiak_____   Juneau _____

Fairbanks _____

Barrow_____

2. Which is coldest? (Circle the correct answer.)

Barrow or Kodiak   Nome or Juneau

Fairbanks or Anchorage   Barrow or Nome

3. Will you be able to build a snowman in Kodiak? (Check one.)

_____ Yes   _____ No

Create the Wind

Hot Air Spirals

Using the pattern below, create two different types of hot-air spirals.

Spiral 1

Materials

- markers
- scissors
- thread
- paper
- pattern

Directions

1. Trace, color, and cut out the pattern below.
2. Poke a hole in the center of the spiral between the XX.
3. Cut a piece of thread about 8" (20 cm) long.
4. Poke the thread through the hole and knot it.
5. Hold the spiral by the thread. Stand still. What happens?
6. Hold the spiral above a heat register. If hot air is blowing, how is the spiral's movement different than if there is only cool air?

Spiral 2

Materials

- lamp
- pencils
- scissors
- paper
- patterns

Directions

1. Turn on the lamp.
2. Trace the pattern on the right.
3. Make a small bump on the XX.
4. Hold a pencil just above the light bulb. (Don't burn yourself.)
5. Balance the XX mark of the spiral on the end of the pencil.

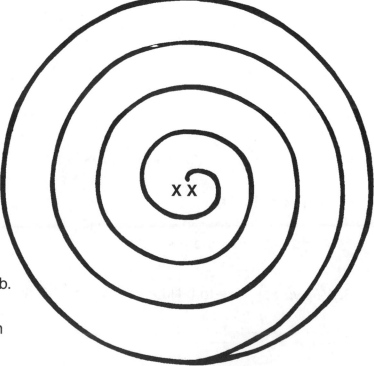

High or Low?

A barometer measures how much the air is pushing down. In wet weather, the air pushes down a little. This is called low pressure. In dry weather, the air presses down a lot. This is called high pressure. A barometer can help you forecast the weather.

Materials

- round balloon
- straw
- jar with wide mouth
- tape
- strong elastic band
- paper and pen

Directions

1. Working with a partner have one partner stretch the balloon by blowing it several times.

2. Cut off the neck by cutting the balloon in half. Throw the neck away.

3. Ask your partner to help you stretch the balloon over the mouth of the jar.

4. Fasten it with the elastic band.

5. Tape the straw onto the balloon "lid" as shown.

6. Cut out a square of paper a little taller than your jar.

7. Mark the paper as shown.

8. Tape the paper to the wall.

9. Place your jar beside the paper.

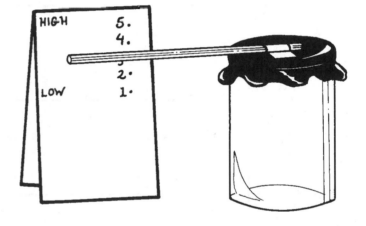

Check your barometer each morning, using the chart on page 122 to record information. Did the straw move? Why?

_____

_____

_____

_____

_____

High or Low? *(cont.)*

Record the barometric pressure.

1. Check your barometer every day at the same time.
2. Record your findings below.
3. What kind of weather makes the straw point the highest?
4. What kind of weather makes the straw point the lowest?

Day	Up (↑) or Down (↓)	Weather

Science Trivia

1. What system of the body is made of the brain, the spinal cord, and the nerves?

_____

2. What comet is visible every 76 years? _____

3. In what three forms can matter exist?_____

4. What instrument is used to measure air pressure? _____

5. What do we call the dirty haze that forms when air pollution combines with moisture in

   the air?_____

6. What part of the body is sometimes called the "funny bone"? _____

7. What substance gives plants their green color? _____

8. What do we call the energy of motion?_____

9. What happens if Earth's crust moves suddenly along a fault? _____

   _____

10. What type of animal eats only meat? _____

11. What do all living things inhale during respiration?_____

12. Which is warmer—tepid or hot water? _____

13. What tube connects the mouth and the stomach? _____

14. What do we call pieces of stone that enter Earth's atmosphere?_____

   _____

15. What is the opening at the top of a volcano called? _____

More Science Trivia

1. What instrument is used to measure temperature? _____

2. What are animals without backbones called? _____

3. With what does a fish breathe? _____

4. In what sea creatures are pearls found? _____

5. What instrument is used to view things that are far away? _____

6. Which is the sixth planet from the sun? _____

7. What animal uses its odor as a defense? _____

8. How many legs does a spider have? _____

9. What birds can fly backwards? _____

10. What is another name for very low clouds? _____

11. What is a frog called when it still has gills? _____

12. Which mammals can fly? _____

13. What is a group of fish called? _____

14. What is another name for a mushroom? _____

15. What do we call the ends of a magnet? _____

Trivia Challenge

1. What system of the human body is made up of blood, blood vessels, and the heart?

   _____

2. Name the brightest planet.

   _____

3. Are reptiles warm- or cold-blooded?

   _____

4. What two names are given to the sun's energy?

   _____

5. Which human bone is most frequently broken?

   _____

6. If a temperature is 32 degrees Farenheit, what is the Celsius temperature?

   _____

7. What *Apollo II* assistant minded the store while Armstrong and Aldrin made history?

   _____

8. What type of climate is hot or warm all year round?

   _____

9. What liquid metal is used in thermometers?

   _____

10. Name the brightest star in the sky.

    _____

11. How many satellites travel around Mars?

    _____

12. Name the largest marsupial.

    _____

13. Which chamber of the human heart pumps blood to most of the body?

    _____

14. What is the opening at the top of a volcano called?

    _____

15. What type of animal eats only plants?

    _____

Science True or False

Before each of the following statements, circle **T** if the statement is true or **F** if the statement is false. On the lines below, explain the "false" responses.

1.   T   F   A telescope is used to view things that are far away.

2.   T   F   The color red is a primary color.

3.   T   F   All insects have six legs.

4.   T   F   Sir Issac Newton discovered gravity by watching an apple fall.

5.   T   F   The smallest bird in the world is the hummingbird.

6.   T   F   The moon gives off its own light.

7.   T   F   All dinosaurs were carnivores.

8.   T   F   The fastest land animal is the African cheetah.

9.   T   F   There are 100 planets in our solar system.

10. T   F   Spiders have eight legs.

_____

_____

_____

_____

_____

_____

_____

_____

_____

_____

_____

_____

_____

More Science True or False

Before each of the following statements, circle **T** if the statement is true or **F** if the statement is false. On the lines below, explain the "false" responses.

1.   T   F   Grownups have a total of 32 permanent teeth.

2.   T   F   The first person to walk on the moon was Neil Armstrong.

3.   T   F   Whales can stay under water for more than an hour.

4.   T   F   The sun is a planet.

5.   T   F   A baby goat is called a kid.

6.   T   F   A dolphin is a fish.

7.   T   F   The diamond is the hardest of all minerals.

8.   T   F   A ladybird is a female bird.

9.   T   F   The air we breathe is mostly nitrogen.

10. T   F   In a lunar eclipse, the moon is between the earth and the sun.

_____

_____

_____

_____

_____

_____

_____

_____

_____

_____

_____

Scientific Names

Many of the words that we use in science come from the names of inventors, discoverers, and researchers. For example, when you look at a container of pasteurized milk, you know that the milk went through a process called pasteurization developed by Louis Pasteur, a French bacteriologist.

Here are some more science words that come from scientists' names.   Can you match the words to the scientists?

_____ 1. Watt	A. Charles Richter, American seismologist
_____ 2. Celsius	B. Alessandro Volta, Italian physicist
_____ 3. Volt	C. Rudolf Diesel, German automotive engineer
_____ 4. Ohm	D. Andre Ampere, French physicist
_____ 5. Richter scale	E. Georg Simon Ohm, German physicist
_____ 6. Diesel	F. James Watt, Scottish engineer and inventor
_____ 7. Ampere	G. Anders Celsius, Swedish astronomer and inventor
_____ 8. Fahrenheit	H. Alexander Bell, American inventor of the telephone
_____ 9. Mach number	I. Gabriel Fahrenheit, German physicist
_____ 10. Decibel	J. Ernst Mach, Austrian philosopher and physicist

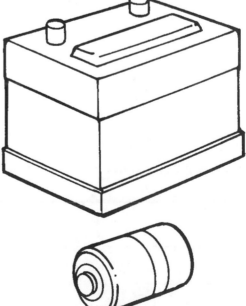

Science Clues

Using the clues, fill in the missing letters to spell the science words.

1. This is someone who travels into space.   ____st____on____ut

2. This is round, and we live on it.   e____rt____

3. These are often fluffy, and they float in the sky.   ____lo____ ____s

4. When some animals sleep through the winter,
    they do this.   h____ber____ate

5. This creature may buzz or crawl.   in____e____t

6. Light is reflected from this at night.   m____ ____n

7. When one of these comes, the wind blows
    very hard.   ____urr____c____n____

8. When this happens, everything gets wet.   ____ai____

9. When we eat, the food goes into this organ.   st____ ____ach

10. To see very small things, scientists use this.   ____icr____ ____co____e

11. These are pretty, and they smell pleasant.   f____ow____ ____s

12. This is very cold and white.   ____no____

13. To determine your temperature, you
    need this.   t____ ____rmo____et____ ____

14. These animals do not lay eggs.   m____ ____m ____l____

15. This force keeps us on the planet Earth.   ____ra____i____ ____

Science ABCs

Without using a dictionary, how many words can you list to complete the chart below? Each word must begin with the letter of the alphabet given. There are many different answers for some, but not all spaces have an answer.

	Animals	Vegetables	Minerals
A			
B			
C			
D			
E			
F			
G			
H			
I			
J			
K			
L			
M			
N			
O			
P			
Q			
R			
S			
T			
U			
V			
W			
X			
Y			
Z			

Matching the Sciences

Cut out the cards on this page and the pages that follow. Turn them facedown. Play by yourself or with a partner. Turn over two cards. If the science word matches the science field (Life Science or Earth Science), take the two cards. If not, turn them over and try again.

Life Science	Earth Science
Life Science	Earth Science
Life Science	Earth Science
Life Science	Earth Science
Life Science	Earth Science

Matching the Sciences *(cont.)*

Life Science	Earth Science
Life Science	Earth Science
Life Science	**earthquake**
digestion	**tornado**
skeleton	**larynx**

Matching the Sciences (cont.)

clay	cell
diamond	hibernation
climate	eardrum
gravity	nervous system
volcano	blood

Insect Bingo

Materials:

- Insect Bingo card with FREE spot (page 135)

- insect game pieces—11 different kinds (page 136 and 137); (30 pieces altogether—see page 137 for list)

- insect calling cards (page 137)

- instructions

Directions for Game Construction

1. Reproduce the insect game pieces. Each player will need 24 insect pictures. Color the pictures if desired. Cut out 24 insect squares.

2. Reproduce the insect bingo card, one for each player. Mount it on cardboard or heavy paper. Have players glue or paste game pieces in each square, except for the FREE spot. Make sure that each column has no duplicate bugs! (**Example:** If two butterflies are under the B column, this would be wrong. However, you could put one butterfly in each of the columns B, I, N, G, O. This would be acceptable.)

3. Reproduce the insect calling card. You will need two sheets. Mount one on tagboard or heavy construction paper. The other sheet may be glued or pasted on cardboard, tagboard, or construction paper. Cut out each calling piece from the first sheet. These will be the bingo calling pieces. The other sheet will be used to keep track of the insects called.

4. To have your game pieces last longer, laminate cards, calling pieces, etc.

How to Play the Game

1. Distribute bingo markers to each player (beans, buttons, and corn kernels work well). Each player should have an insect bingo card.

2. Someone needs to be a caller. The caller draws a calling piece from a box, hat, or other container (**Example:** G-grasshopper). If a player has on his or her card a beetle under the G-column, he or she may place a marker on it. The caller then places the calling piece on the caller's card under the appropriate column. The caller continues drawing until a player has bingo! Bingo is reached when a player's card has a column (either horizontal, vertical, or diagonal through FREE) filled with markers. The player then shouts "BINGO!"

Insect Bingo *(cont.)*

Card

B	I	N	G	O
		FREE		

Insect Bingo (cont.)

Game Pieces

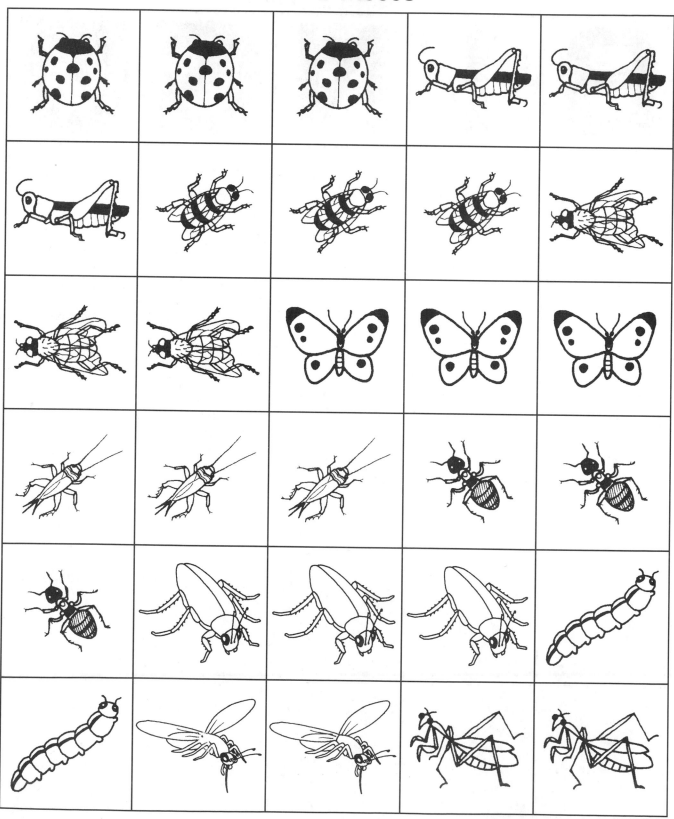

Insect Bingo *(cont.)*

B	I	N	G	O
Ant	Ant	Ant	Ant	Ant
Bee	Bee	Bee	Bee	Bee
Butterfly	Butterfly	Butterfly	Butterfly	Butterfly
Caterpillar	Caterpillar	Caterpillar	Caterpillar	Caterpillar
Cockroach	Cockroach	Cockroach	Cockroach	Cockroach
Cricket	Cricket	Cricket	Cricket	Cricket
Fly	Fly	Fly	Fly	Fly
Grasshopper	Grasshopper	Grasshopper	Grasshopper	Grasshopper
Ladybug	Ladybug	Ladybug	Ladybug	Ladybug
Mosquito	Mosquito	Mosquito	Mosquito	Mosquito
Praying Mantis	Praying Mantis	Praying Mantis	Praying Mantis	Praying Mantis

Vertebrate and Invertebrate Animals

All animals are classified into two major groups: vertebrate and invertebrate. Vertebrate animals include all animals that have a backbone or spine. Invertebrate animals include all animals without a backbone or spine. Classify the animals below into vertebrate or invertebrate groups, then into a subgroup, then by the name of the animal, and finally by the picture of the animal. (Cut out the picture and glue it to the chart.) Use the words from the word box to help identify the animals.

Word Box

Animal Subgroups		Animal Names	
• mammal	• insect	• dragonfly	• conch
• bird	• snail	• earthworm	• snake
• reptile	• spider	• thousand leg	• raccoon
• dinosauria	• crustacesan	• brown spider	• catfish
• fish	• worm	• protoceratops	• lobster
• amphibian	• centipede/ millipede	• duck	• frog

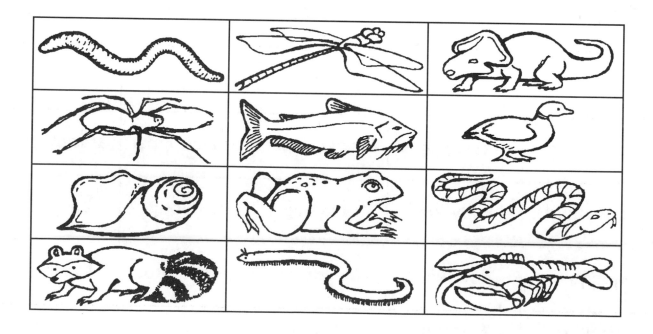

Vertebrate and Invertebrate Animals Chart

Major Group	Subgroup	Name	Picture

Social Studies

Famous Names

How many of the names in the box below do you recognize? Do you know what each one is noted for? Use resource books to help you find out. Then write the proper name beside each phrase.

1. _____ world's first female physician

2. _____ wrote "The Battle Hymn of the Republic"

3. _____ invented sleeping cars for trains

4. _____ invented the mechanical reaper

5. _____ invented the phonograph

6. _____ baseball's inventor

7. _____ poet; wrote "Leaves of Grass"

8. _____ circus–"The Greatest Show on Earth"

9. _____ invented the telephone

10. _____ invented the cable car

11. _____ inventor of the elevator

12. _____ made air brakes for passenger trains

13. _____ founder of the first successful five and dime store

14. _____ invented the telegraph

15. _____ wrote *The Adventures of Tom Sawyer*

Cyrus McCormick	Alexander Graham Bell
Julia Ward Howe	Abner Doubleday
George Westinghouse	Walt Whitman
F. W. Woolworth	A. S. Hallidie
Mark Twain	Thomas Edison
P. T. Barnum	E. G. Otis
Samuel Morse	G. M. Pullman
Elizabeth Blackwell	

Inventors and Their Inventions

Using items in the Invention Box below, write each invention next to the name of the person who is responsible for it.

1. George Eastman _____

2. George M. Pullman _____

3. Johannes Gutenberg _____

4. Guglielmo Marconi _____

5. Charles Goodyear _____

6. Clarence Birdseye _____

7. Alfred B. Nobel _____

8. Alexander Graham Bell _____

9. Benjamin Franklin _____

10. John Deere _____

11. Wright Brothers _____

12. Thomas Edison _____

13. Henry Ford _____

14. Eli Whitney _____

15. Elias Howe _____

Invention Box

cotton gin	dynamite	vulcanization of rubber
electric light	steel plow	first successful airplane
sewing machine	Kodak camera	printing from movable type
bifocal glasses	wireless telegraph	assembly line method of production
telephone	railroad sleeping car	quick-freezing process of preserving food

Louis Braille's Code
(Born January 4, 1809)

Louis Braille was a Frenchman who invented a raised dot writing system for the blind. A special typewriter presses against paper to form the different dot sequences.

Use the Braille letter dot code to write and read the messages.

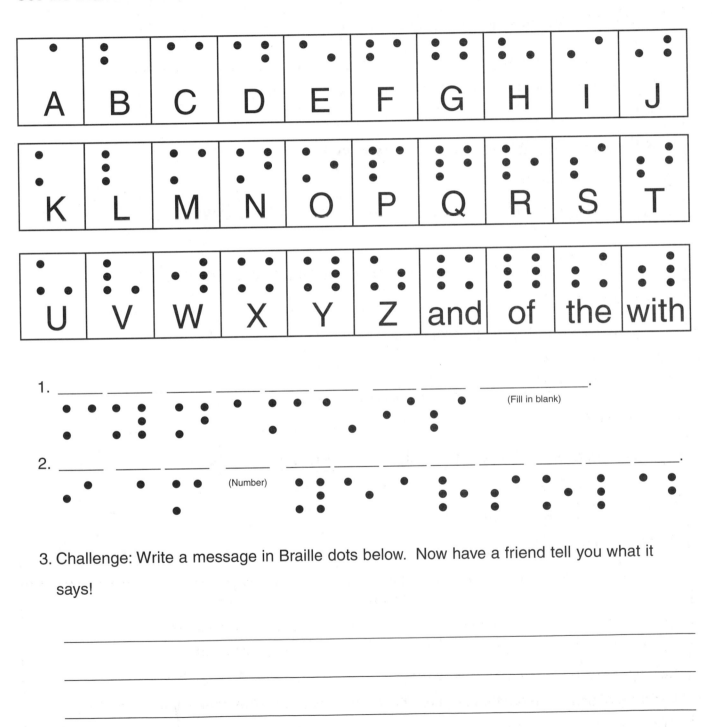

1. ____ ____ ____ ____ ____ ____ _____ .
                                                 (Fill in blank)

2. ____ ____ ____ ____ ____ ____ ____ ____ .
                    (Number)

3. Challenge: Write a message in Braille dots below. Now have a friend tell you what it

   says!

   _____

   _____

   _____

Excellent Explorers

Discovering the names of these famous explorers is as easy as A, B, C! Use the clues below to fill in their names. All the As, Bs, and Cs have been written in for you.

1. In 1492 he sailed the ocean blue.

    • C ___ ___ ___ ___ B ___ ___

2. This American naval man went to the North and South Poles.

    • B ___ ___ ___

3. This Spanish explorer conquered the Aztecs.

    • C ___ ___ ___ ___ ___

4. She was the first female to fly solo over the Atlantic Ocean.

    • ___ A ___ ___ A ___ ___

5. This man studied evolution by observing Galapagos turtles.

    • ___ A ___ ___ ___ ___

6. This Portugese explorer circled the world.

    • ___ A ___ ___ ___ ___ A ___

7. This modern-day explorer's territory was the sea.

    • C ___ ___ ___ ___ ___ A ___

8. This Spanish explorer is said to have discovered the Pacific.

    • B A ___ B ___ A

9. He conquered the Incas in Peru.

    • ___ ___ ___ A ___ ___ ___

10. This French explorer found the St. Lawrence Seaway.

    • C A ___ ___ ___ ___ ___

11. This man was the first person to walk on the moon.

    • A ___ ___ ___ ___ ___ ___ ___ ___

12. This English navigator has a river in New York named after him.

    • ___ ___ ___ ___ ___ ___

Presidential First Names

Listed below are some last names of former presidents. Write each president's first name on the blank.

1. _____ Adams

2. _____ Eisenhower

3. _____ Reagan

4. _____ Jefferson

5. _____ Nixon

6. _____ Lincoln

7. _____ Carter

8. _____ Hoover

9. _____ Roosevelt

10. _____ Washington

11. _____ Coolidge

12. _____ Cleveland

13. _____ Grant

14. _____ Taylor

15. _____ Harrison

16. _____ Truman

17. _____ Buchanan

18. _____ Polk

19. _____ Garfield

20. _____ Johnson

Famous Women

Match these women to their major accomplishments. Put the letter of the accomplishment before the corresponding name.

_____ 1. Harriet Tubman

_____ 2. Harriet Beecher Stowe

_____ 3. Grandma Moses

_____ 4. Juliette Gordon Low

_____ 5. Shirley Chisholm

_____ 6. Pearl S. Buck

_____ 7. Mary McLeod Bethune

_____ 8. Clara Barton

_____ 9. Louisa May Alcott

_____ 10. Susan B. Anthony

_____ 11. Jane Addams

_____ 12. Amelia Earhart

_____ 13. Helen Hayes

_____ 14. Helen Keller

_____ 15. Victoria C. Woodhull

A. social worker and humanitarian

B. primitive painter

C. novelist and reformer

D. stage and screen actress

E. author of *The Good Earth*

F. aviator

G. author of *Little Women*

H. educator who worked to improve educational opportunities for blacks

I. significant "conductor" of the Underground Railroad

J. first woman to run for president of the U.S.

K. first African American woman in the U.S. Congress

L. founded the Girl Scouts of America

M. founded the American Red Cross

N. overcame physical handicaps; helped thousands of handicapped people lead fuller lives

O. reformer and leader in the American women's suffrage movement

Famous People

Can you identify the names of these twelve famous people from American history using the parts of their first and last names shown in each box?

1.
__ | A U | __
__ __ | V E | __ __

7.
__ | E O | __ __ __
__ __ __ | H I | __ __ __ __

2.
__ | B R | __ __ __ __
__ | I N | __ __ __ __

8.
__ __ | O M | __ __
__ __ | I S | __ __

3.
__ __ __ | E R | __
__ . | L E | __

9.
__ __ __ | J A | __ __ __
__ __ __ | N K | __ __ __

4.
__ | O U | __ __ __ __
__ __ | C A | __ __ __ __ __

10.
__ | E I | __
__ __ __ | S T | __ __ __ __

5.
__ __ | R R | __ __ __
__ | U B | __ __ __

11.
__ | M E | __ __ __
__ | A R | __ __ __ __

6.
__ | O H | __ __ __
__ __ | P L | __ __ __ __ __

12.
__ | E T | __ __
__ | O S | __

Countries of South America

All the consonants are missing in the names of the South American countries below. Use a map of South America to help you fill in the missing letters.

1. ___ U ___ A ___ A

2. A ___ ___ E ___ ___ I ___ A

3. ___ E ___ E ___ U E ___ A

4. ___ O ___ I ___ I A

5. U ___ U ___ U A ___

6. ___ ___ E ___ ___ ___ ___ U I A ___ A

7. ___ U ___ I ___ A ___ E

8. ___ ___ ___ A ___ I ___

9. ___ E ___ U

10. ___ ___ ___ I ___ E

11. ___ A ___ A ___ U A ___

12. ___ O ___ O ___ ___ I A

13. E ___ U A ___ O ___

Test Your Map Skills

Using a globe and the map of the United States of America on page 151, respond correctly to the following questions.

1. Which state is the farthest south?

   _____

2. Which state is the largest?

   _____

3. Which state is the smallest?

   _____

4. Which states border Iowa?

   _____

5. Which states are directly north of the Oklahoma border?

   _____

6. Which states have shorelines on the Gulf of Mexico?

   _____

7. Which state is made up of eight islands?

   _____

8. Which state is farther west—Colorado or Idaho?

   _____

9. What state is directly south of Wisconsin?

   _____

10. Which state is farther north—New York or Virginia?

   _____

Test Your Map Skills *(cont.)*

11. Which states border California?

_____

12. Which states begin with the letter M?

_____

13. Which states have shorelines on the Atlantic Ocean?

_____

14. Which states have shorelines on the Pacific Ocean?

_____

15. Which states have shorelines on the Great Lakes?

_____

16. Which state reaches farthest west?

_____

17. Which state is the farthest north?

_____

18. Which states border on Mexico?

_____

19. Which states border on Canada?

_____

20. Which island has the largest United States city on it?

_____

Test Your Map Skills *(cont.)*

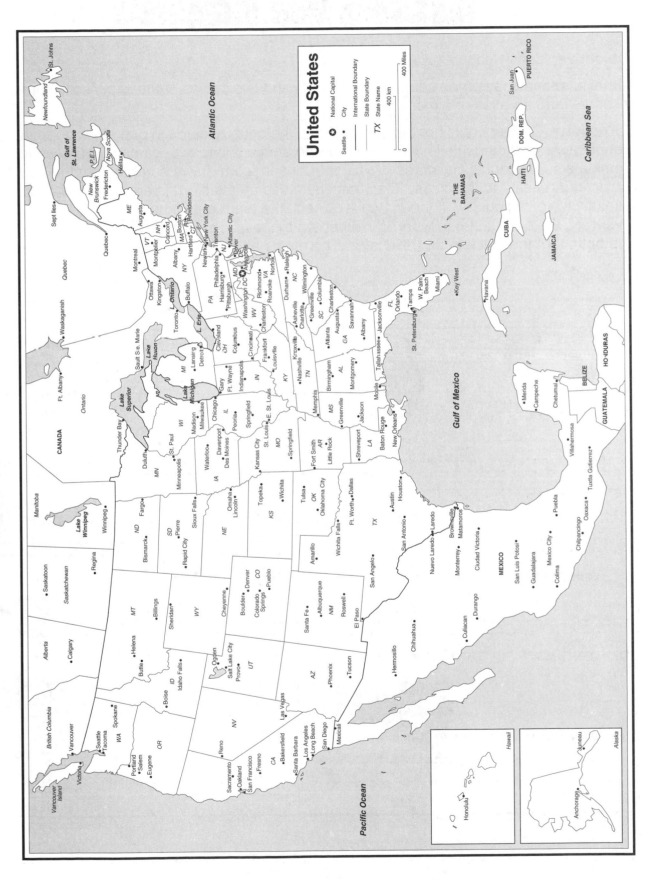

Matching World Capitals

Objective: identify capital cities of the world

Materials: one copy of the country name cards and two copies of the capital city cards, scissors, and an atlas or almanac

Directions: Cut out copies of the cards. Place the country cards in one stack and place each set of capital city cards in its own stack. Divide students into two teams. Give each team a complete set of capital city cards. A member of one team draws a name from the country cards and reads it to the class. Team members use an atlas or almanac to try to match the capital city to its country. If the match is correct, the team gets a point. If the match is incorrect, the other team may try. If neither team guesses correctly, the country card goes to the bottom of the stack to be used later. The teams alternate turns.

Country Cards

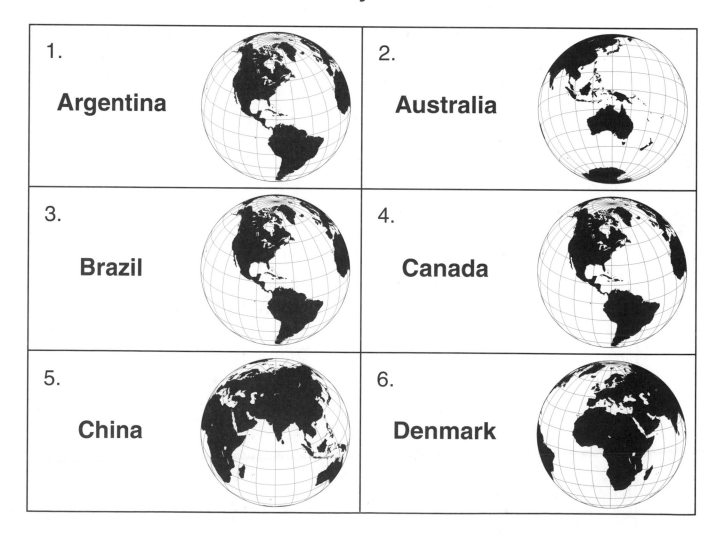

1. Argentina	2. Australia
3. Brazil	4. Canada
5. China	6. Denmark

Matching World Capitals *(cont.)*

Country Cards *(cont.)*

7. **France**	8. **Germany**
9. **India**	10. **Iran**
11. **Iraq**	12. **Israel**
13. **Japan**	14. **Poland**
15. **Russia**	16. **United States**

Matching World Capitals *(cont.)*

Capital City Cards

a.
 **Baghdad**

b.
 **Beijing**

c.
 **Berlin**

d.
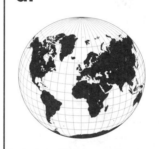 **Brasilia**

e.
 **Buenos Aires**

f.
 **Canberra**

g.
 **Copenhagen**

h.
 **Jerusalem**

Matching World Capitals *(cont.)*

Capital City Cards *(cont.)*

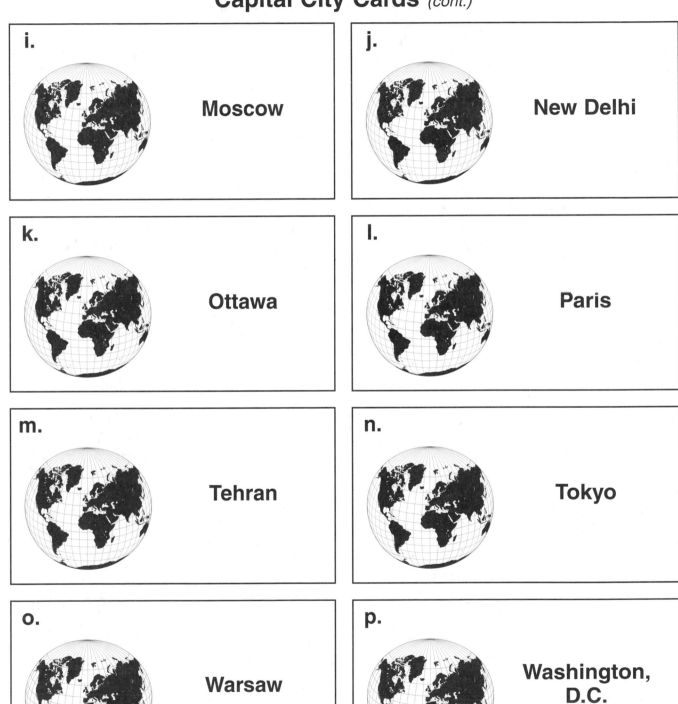

i. Moscow

j. New Delhi

k. Ottawa

l. Paris

m. Tehran

n. Tokyo

o. Warsaw

p. Washington, D.C.

Where Is It?

Using an atlas or globe, find the latitudes and longitudes of the following cities.

1. Des Moines, Iowa _____

2. London, England _____

3. Guadalajara, Mexico _____

4. Oslo, Norway _____

5. Athens, Greece _____

Using an atlas or globe, find the following cities by their latitudes and longitudes.

City	Latitude	Longitude
6. _____	34° S	18° E
7. _____	33° N	117° W
8. _____	49° N	2° E
9. _____	44° N	79° W
10. _____	52° N	13° E

Using the map on page 157 as reference, write the name of continent that each country is located on.

11. Mexico_____   16. Kenya _____

12. China_____   17. Morocco _____

13. Brazil_____   18. Iceland_____

14. Australia _____   19. Argentina_____

15. Italy _____   20. Thailand _____

Where Is It? *(cont.)*

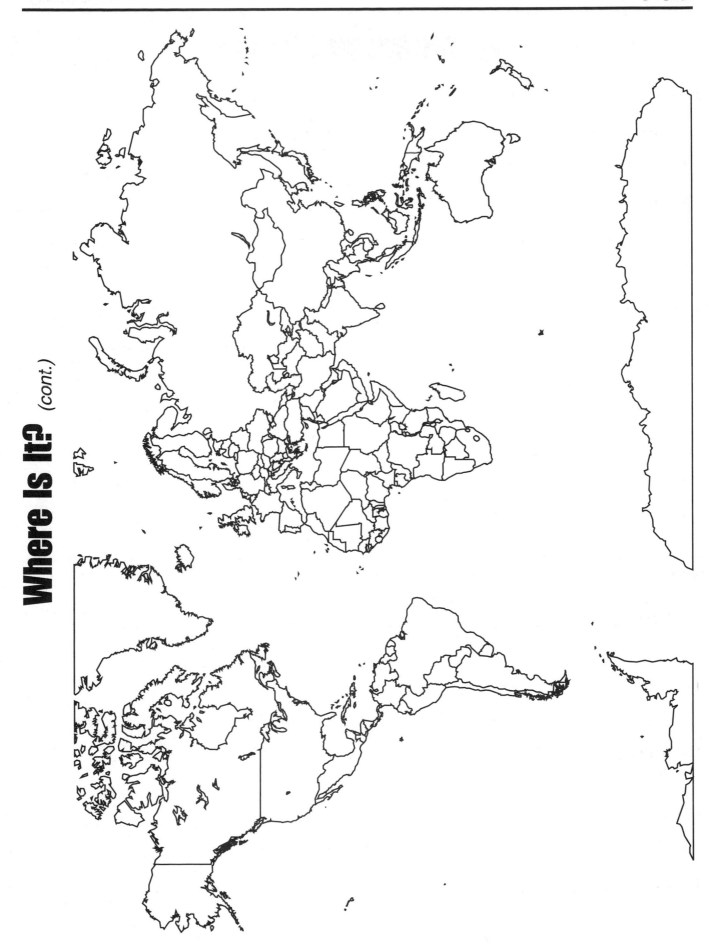

Black History Trivia

1. Who is Harry Belafonte?

   _____

2. Did Mary McLeod Bethune work in the field of education?

   _____

3. Andrew Young served as the mayor of what city?

   _____

4. Who founded the NAACP?

   _____

5. What is slavery?

   _____

6. Where is Harlem?

   _____

7. What is an abolitionist?

   _____

8. What did Thurgood Marshall accomplish?

   _____

9. What is segregation?

   _____

10. Did blacks fight in the Civil War?

    _____

11. What sport did Arthur Ashe play?

    _____

12. What was the Emancipation Proclamation?

    _____

13. Who was Jackie Robinson?

    _____

14. Who is Guion Bluford, Jr.?

    _____

15. Were Matthew Henson and Estevancio both black explorers?

    _____

American Holidays Trivia

1. Which two U.S. presidents' birthdays do we celebrate in February?

   _____

2. When is Independence Day?

   _____

3. In what month is Thanksgiving celebrated?

   _____

4. When do we observe Veterans Day?

   _____

5. What holiday is celebrated on the first Monday in September?

   _____

6. Why do we celebrate Memorial Day?

   _____

7. Which holiday is observed on the second Monday in October?

   _____

8. What famous civil rights activist is honored in January?

   _____

9. On what day is the above activist honored?

   _____

10. On what holiday is a famous parade honoring Irish ancestry held in New York City?

    _____

11. What holiday is celebrated on the second Sunday in September and honors the oldest
    family members?

    _____

12. What current holiday was originally called Constitution Day?

    _____

Social Studies Trivia

1. On which continent is Canada located?_____

2. In traveling north, what direction is to the right? _____

3. On the American flag, are there more red or white stripes? _____

4. What is the longest river in the U.S.?_____

5. What does "N" on a map normally represent? _____

6. Who invented the telephone?_____

7. What is a book of maps called?_____

8. Name the highest mountain in the world._____

9. What do you call a piece of land surrounded with water on all sides?

    _____

10. Name the three ships Columbus took on his famous journey?

    _____

11. On what mountain are four famous presidents' faces carved?

    _____

12. Name the five Great Lakes. _____

    _____

13. Of England, Australia, Peru, and Canada, which nation does not have English as a

    national language? _____

14. Name the ocean west of North America. _____

15. What is the capital of Hawaii? _____

More Social Studies Trivia

1. What does one call a government ruled by a king or queen?

   _____

2. Which two countries fought in the War of 1812?

   _____

3. Name the largest African desert.

   _____

4. Across which continent does the Amazon river flow?

   _____

5. Which country lies north of Germany and south of Norway?

   _____

6. Who was the captain of the *Mayflower*?

   _____

7. Of which country is Havana the capital?

   _____

8. What Spanish leader led the conquest of the ancient Aztec people?

   _____

9. To what mountain range does Mt. Everest belong?

   _____

10. Alaska was purchased by the United States from what country?

    _____

11. What type of map shows elevations and contours?

    _____

12. Along the shore of which continent lies the Great Barrier Reef?

    _____

13. During what years was World War I fought?

    _____

14. How many provinces and territories are in Canada?

    _____

15. Name the world's most populous country.

    _____

This Map Is Making Me Hungry!

Many foods are named for the place where they were first made. Other foods share their names with places in the world. Read the following clues to help find the location of these yummy place names.

1. It is a kind of mustard and a city of Europe.

   Where do you go to find Dijon? _____

2. It is a kind of sandwich and a city of Europe.

   Where do you go to find Hamburg? _____

3. It is a pepper sauce and a state in North America.

   Where do you go to find Tabasco?_____

4. It is a red wine and a city in Western Europe.

   Where do you go to find Bordeaux? _____

5. It is a cold cut and a city in Europe.

   Where do you go to find Bologna?_____

6. They are two kinds of cheese and two cities in Europe.

   Where do you go to find Gouda and Edam? _____

7. It is a kind of orange, and cities in Europe and the U.S.A. are named for it.

   Where do you go to find Valencia? _____

8. An American might call it a hot dog, and it is a city in Europe.

   Where do you go to find Frankfurt? _____

9. It is a brand of chocolate and a city in the U.S.A.

   Where do you go to find Hershey? _____

10. It is a cheese and a village in Europe.

    Where do you go to find Cheddar? _____

11. It is a hot southwestern dish and a country.

    Where do you go to find Chile? _____

12. It is two slices of bread with ham, cheese, etc., in the middle and a borough in Europe.

    Where do you go to find Sandwich? _____

13. It is a citrus fruit and a city in Western Europe.

    Where do you go to find Orange? _____

14. It is usually part of the Thanksgiving feast and also a country.

    Where do you go to find Turkey? _____

15. It is a kind of steak and a plain in Europe.

    Where do you go to find Salisbury?_____

Place Names of the World

When people moved from place to place in the world, they often gave the new area where they settled names from the "old country." Listed below are cities and countries in Europe that were used as place names in the United States. Use an atlas, geographical dictionary, or reference books to finish the chart. In some instances, the word "New" precedes the American place name.

European City, Country, or District	City in the United States	State
1. York, England		
2. Cambridge, England		
3. Lincoln, England		
4. Plymouth, England		
5. Salisbury, England		
6. Reading, England		
7. Bern, Switzerland		
8. Birmingham, England		
9. Rome, Italy		
10. Paris, France		
11. Saint Petersburg, Russia		
12. Manchester, England		
13. Athens, Greece		
14. Valencia, Spain		
15. Orleans, France		
16. Waterloo, France		
17. Memphis, Greece		
18. Odessa, Russia		
19. Cleveland, England		
20. Frankfurt, Germany*		

Spelling for American city is slightly different.

Nicknames and Capitals

Use a reference book to locate the nickname and the capital of each of the states listed below.

State	Nickname	Capital
1. Illinois		
2. Utah		
3. West Virginia		
4. Texas		
5. Michigan		
6. Delaware		
7. Kentucky		
8. Alaska		
9. Vermont		
10. Rhode Island		
11. North Dakota		
12. New York		
13. Georgia		
14. Tennessee		
15. Wisconsin		
16. Kansas		
17. Indiana		
18. Connecticut		
19. Washington		
20. California		
21. New Mexico		
22. Minnesota		
23. Pennsylvania		
24. Mississippi		
25. Wyoming		

Puzzled About the States?

Identify the shapes of states used to make the pictures below. Make your own puzzle and challenge a friend to identify the states you have used. Use the map found on page 151 as reference.

Around the World

This game has 45 cards that name countries of the world. Players must name the continent on which each country is located.

Objective: to practice and reinforce knowledge of world countries and their continents

Materials

- card stock of any color to print game card pages and to mount rules and answer key
- laminating materials

Construction

1. Print the game card pages on colored card stock. Laminate the pages and cut the cards apart.

2. Trim the rules box and answer key on page 299. Mount on card stock of same color as used for game cards. Laminate them.

Rules for "Around The World"

This game is for two to four players and one scorekeeper. Paper and pencil are needed for keeping score.

1. Scorekeeper shuffles the game cards and spreads cards face down.

2. Player to the left of scorekeeper goes first. Play moves to the left.

3. First player turns over the top card and reads the card number and name of the country aloud. The player attempts to tell the continent on which that country is located.

4. Scorekeeper checks answer key.

   Correct answer: Win 2 points. Card goes to discard pile. Next player's turn.

   Incorrect answer: Lose 2 points. Card is shuffled back into card pile. Next player's turn.

5. When all cards are used or when game time is over, the player with the most points is the winner.

Around the World *(cont.)*

1. **ARGENTINA**	2. **BELGIUM**	3. **BOLIVIA**
4. **BRAZIL**	5. **CANADA**	6. **CHILE**
7. **CHINA**	8. **CUBA**	9. **EGYPT**
10. **FRANCE**	11. **GERMANY**	12. **GREECE**
13. **INDIA**	14. **IRAN**	15. **IRAQ**

Around the World *(cont.)*

16. ISRAEL	17. IRELAND	18. ENGLAND
19. ITALY	20. JAPAN	21. KENYA
22. NORTH KOREA	23. SOUTH KOREA	24. KUWAIT
25. LIBYA	26. MADAGASCAR	27. NETHERLANDS
28. NEW ZEALAND	29. NICARAGUA	30. NIGERIA

Around the World *(cont.)*

31. NORWAY	32. PAKISTAN	33. PERU
34. PHILIPPINES	35. POLAND	36. PORTUGAL
37. SAUDI ARABIA	38. RUSSIA	39. SPAIN
40. SWEDEN	41. SWITZERLAND	42. SYRIA
43. UNITED STATES	44. TURKEY	45. SCOTLAND

My Family Tree

Take this form home and fill in the information you will need for creating your own family tree in the social studies center. You may collect more information than what is asked on this form, if you wish, and even photographs if available.

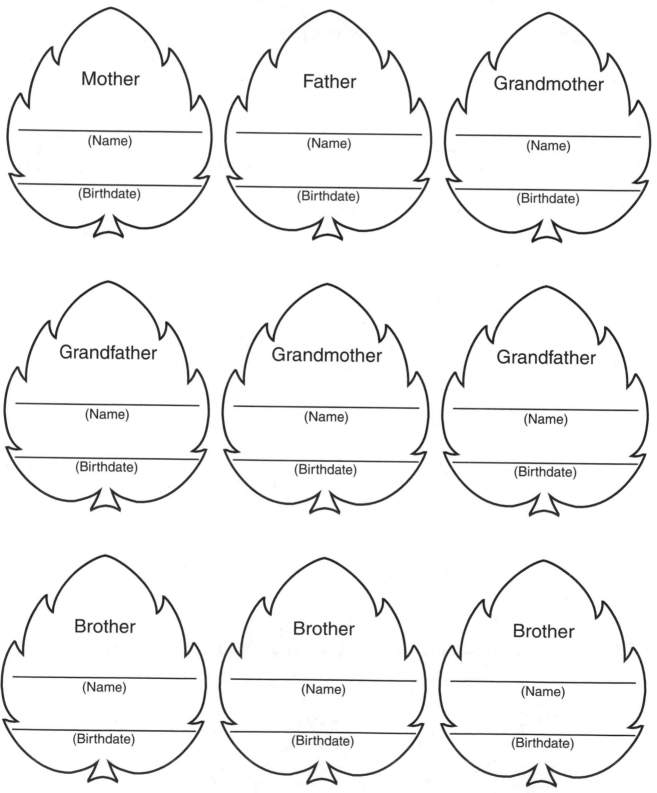

Mother

(Name)

(Birthdate)

Father

(Name)

(Birthdate)

Grandmother

(Name)

(Birthdate)

Grandfather

(Name)

(Birthdate)

Grandmother

(Name)

(Birthdate)

Grandfather

(Name)

(Birthdate)

Brother

(Name)

(Birthdate)

Brother

(Name)

(Birthdate)

Brother

(Name)

(Birthdate)

My Family Tree *(cont.)*

On the leaves below, fill in the information you found. You may make additional leaves by tracing around one of these. If you have photographs or other items to add, you may attach them to additional leaves.

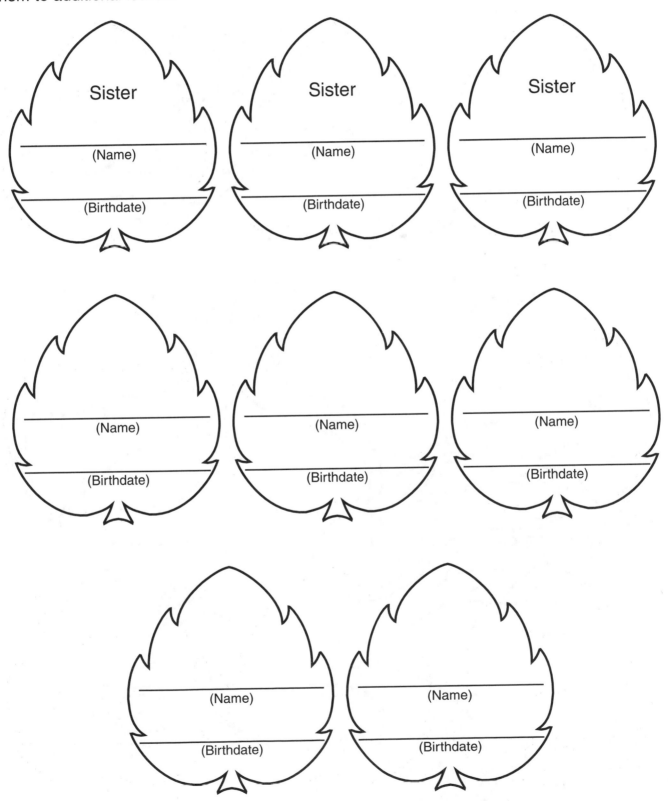

My Family Tree *(cont.)*

Glue pages 172 and 173 together to form your family tree. Glue the leaves from pages 170 and 171 on the branches to complete your tree.

My Family Tree *(cont.)*

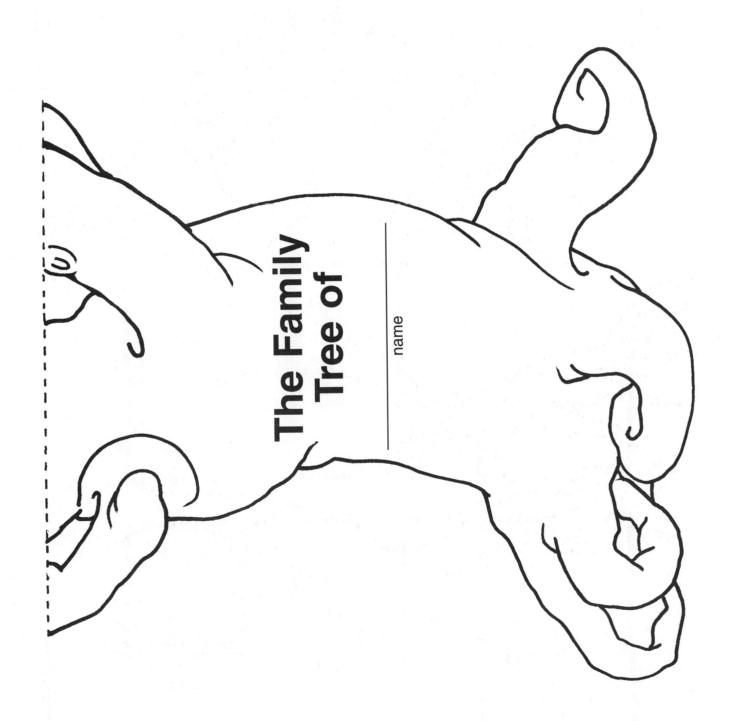

The Family Tree of

_____
name

Patchwork Quilts Kit

The process of quilting (two layers of fabric with wool or loft between and stitched together) has been known since 3000 B.C., and possibly even earlier. Quilted clothing and household goods have been discovered in ancient Egypt, Mongolia, and the Middle East. Knights in the Middle Ages wore quilted clothing under their armor, and a bed quilt, used in the 1300s was found in Sicily. It can be seen in the Victoria and Albert Museum in London. When people came to settle the Western Hemisphere, they brought the art of quilting with them, and soon quilt-making became a very popular activity in America. Quilts were used for warmth on beds, of course, but they were also used for door, window, and floor covers; they were even sometimes used like money to pay bills. Often, quilts are made up of a hodge-podge of scraps of fabric from old, worn clothes; but as the art has evolved, more and more often quilts have been made to be a work of art as well as a family history.

The most basic quilts are made from pieced together geometric shapes in repeating patterns and colors. In your Patchwork Quilts Kit, you will find patterns for many of the shapes commonly used. Trace around these shapes on colored construction paper and cut the shapes you wish to use for your paper patchwork quilt square. You may wish to get ideas by looking at these designs first, and then making some sketches. Try the shapes in various positions to see if the colors and shapes please you. When you have a pattern you like, glue it into place and write your name on the back.

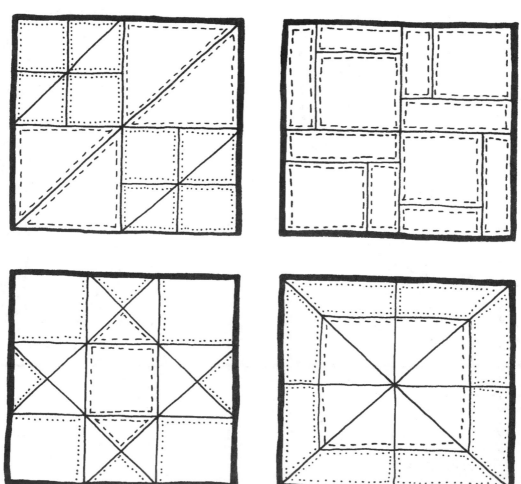

Patchwork Quilts Kit *(cont.)*

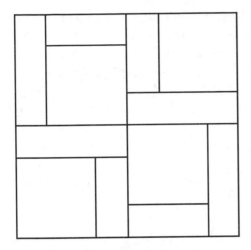

Patience Corner

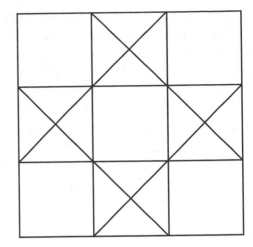

Ohio Star

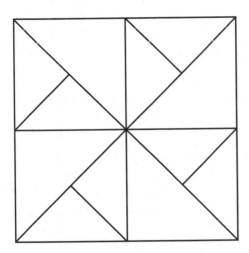

Windmill

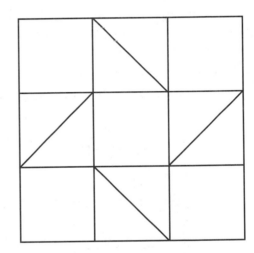

Friendship Star

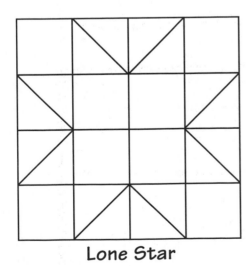

Lone Star

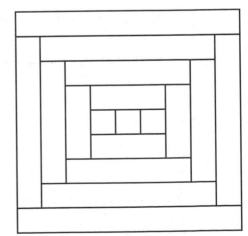

Log Cabin

Patchwork Quilts Kit *(cont.)*

Use the geometric shapes below to create some of the patterns on pages 174 and 175 or use them to create your own design.

Games & Puzzles

You Must Be Joe King!

Below are three common types of jokes. Follow the directions in each section.

Puns

A *pun* is something that is funny because of a play on words, often because one or more of the words have more than one meaning or sound similar to other words. Read the following puns and circle the words that make each a pun.

1. *Mona*: I can't marry you, Jib; you're penniless.

    Jib: That's nothing—the Czar of Russia was Nicholas!

2. Cantaloupe today, lettuce tomorrow.

3. *Diner:* This coffee tastes like mud!

    Waiter: That's funny—it was just ground this morning!

4. It's raining cats and dogs! I just stepped in a poodle.

5. Did you hear about the guy who ate 90 pancakes? How waffle!

Tom Swifties

A *Tom Swifty* is a joke that quotes a person saying something, and the verb or adverb describes how the quotation was said. Read the examples below and then write five Tom Swifties of your own on the back of this paper.

1. "I don't have a fever," he said *cooly*.

2. "I'll pay you one thousand dollars," said the rich woman *grandly*.

3. "I love hot dogs," admitted the girl *frankly*.

4. "I've decided to change your test grade," the teacher *remarked*.

5. "Please pass the sugar," said Jeff *sweetly*.

Daffynitions

Daffynitions are silly definitions for words, based on how they sound literally. Read the following examples and then write the real definitions for the words. Then use five words of your own (or select from the choices below) to write your own daffynitions on the back of this paper.

- boycott: *a bed for a small male child*
- cartoon: *a song sung in an automobile*
- eye dropper: *someone who is very, very careless*
- sweater _____
- paradox_____
- paramedics _____

- grammar _____
- missing _____
- lawsuit_____
- divine_____
- Denise_____
- kidnap _____

Presidential Stumpers

Use the names of the presidents to answer these questions humorously. The first one has been done for you.

1. Which president was the most honest? _____ Truman _____

2. Which president was the slowest? _____

3. Which president was irritated by his child? _____

4. Which president was popular at a service station? _____

5. Which president was the namesake of a popular cat? _____

6. Which president sewed clothing?_____

7. Which president took care of the laundry? _____

8. Which president was helpful in fixing a flat tire? _____

9. Which president was often cold? _____

10. Which president cleaned the carpets?_____

Letter Answers

Use one or two letters of the alphabet to respond to each of the clues. The first one has been done for you.

1.	Not difficult	**EZ**
2.	Cold	_____
3.	Goodbye	_____
4.	Vegetable	_____
5.	Body of water	_____
6.	Girl's name	_____
7.	Exclamation	_____
8.	Organ used for sight	_____
9.	Pronoun	_____
10.	Tent home	_____
11.	Plant or vine	_____
12.	Question	_____
13.	Something to drink	_____
14.	Insect	_____
15.	Radio announcer	_____

More Letter Answers

Use one, two, or three letters of the alphabet to "spell" a word corresponding to each of the following clues. The first one has been done for you.

1. Used in a pool game   Q

2. Happiness   _____

3. A foe   _____

4. Jealousy   _____

5. A woman's name   _____

6. In debt   _____

7. A written composition   _____

8. What makes a movie exciting   _____

9. A boy's name   _____

10. To say good-bye   _____

11. The number after 79   _____

12. A drink, hot or iced   _____

13. An exclamation   _____

14. To be good at something   _____

15. To rot   _____

Which Came First?

Look at the lists below and see if you can determine which comes first. Write the correct order by putting a one, a two, or a three in the space after each one.

1. Hoover _____ Jefferson _____ Lincoln _____

2. 2/5 _____ 1/3 _____ 1/2 _____

3. airplane _____ radio _____ television _____

4. Babe Ruth _____ Michael Jordan _____ Joe Namath _____

5. Civil War _____ Spanish American War _____ Revolutionary War _____

6. Elton John _____ Elvis _____ Beatles _____

7. Industrial Revolution _____ Westward Expansion _____ Space Race _____

8. Michigan _____ Hawaii _____ Massachusetts _____

9. Picasso _____ Michelangelo _____ Van Gogh _____

10. phonograph _____ telephone _____ light bulb _____

11. 6/7 _____ 2/3 _____ 4/5 _____

12. Pearl Harbor _____ Kennedy assassination _____ Great Depression _____

13. first space shuttle flight _____ first man on the moon _____

    Nixon resignation _____

14. Neil Armstrong _____ Sally Ride _____ John Glenn _____

15. Mark Twain _____ Ernest Hemingway _____ William Shakespeare _____

States Ending in "A"

Twenty-one of the fifty states end in the letter "A." Can you find these states in the word
search below? Answers can be found across or down.

Alabama Alaska Arizona *California* Florida Georgia Indiana

West Virginia | **Virginia** | **South Dakota** | **South Carolina**

Iowa Louisiana Minnesota Montana Nebraska **Nevada**

```
N O R T H D A K O T A A L O A
O R L O U I S I A N A I I A L
R W E S T V I R G I N I A K E
T G O N F F L O R I D A N S S
H A I N R O F I L A C N N A K
C A V I R G I N I A W A E R O
A R I Z O N A O A W O I V B N
R M R M I A L A I D A S A E O
O A D O D A A R A N A I D N I
L M I N N E S O T A N U A R R
I A N T I L K A I G R O E G T
N B I A U O A M O H A L K O H
A A A N I L O R A C H T U O S
S L A A I N A V L Y S N N E P
I A S O U T H D A K O T A A C
```

North Carolina North Dakota **Oklahoma** PENNSYLVANIA

Morse Code

Here is what Morse code looks like. It sounds like this: dot = quick sound or tap, dash = longer sound). Using Morse code, write a note to a friend using only the dots and dashes of the code. Be sure to allow enough space between each letter so that the letters don't run into each other.

Morse Code

A ●▬	B ▬●●●	C ▬●▬●	D ▬●●	E ●	F ●●▬●
G ▬▬●	H ●●●●	I ●●	J ●▬▬▬	K ▬●▬	L ●▬●●
M ▬▬	N ▬●	O ▬▬▬	P ●▬▬●	Q ▬▬●▬	R ●▬●
S ●●●	T ▬	U ●●▬	V ●●●▬	W ●▬▬	X ▬●●▬
Y ▬●▬▬	Z ▬▬●●	1 ●▬▬▬▬	2 ●●▬▬▬	3 ●●●▬▬	4 ●●●●▬
5 ●●●●●	6 ▬●●●●	7 ▬▬●●●	8 ▬▬▬●●	9 ▬▬▬▬●	0 ▬▬▬▬▬

period ●▬●▬●▬	comma ▬▬●●▬▬	? ●●▬▬●●	SOS ●●●▬▬▬●●●		Start ▬●▬
End of Message ●▬●▬●		Understand ●▬●		Error ●●●●●●●●	

Coded Message

Circle the correct letter for each problem below. Then, take the circled letter and put it in the corresponding blank in order to reveal a famous saying.

___ ___ ___   ___ ___ ___   ___ ___   ___ ___ ___
7 2 6   8 5 3   11 1   7 2 6

___ ___ ___ ___ ___   ___ ___ ___   ___ ___ ___
9 4 11 3 10   7 2 6   8 5 3

1. If man walked on the moon in 1492, circle S. If not, circle F.

2. If a prairie dog is a dog, circle K. If it is a rodent, circle O.

3. If your father's sister is your aunt, circle N. If not, circle A.

4. If 6 x 9 = 55, circle M. If not, circle H.

5. If antonyms are words that mean the opposite of one another, circle A. If not, circle L.

6. If Brazil is a country in Europe, circle K. If not, circle U.

7. If the capital of Illinois is Springfield, circle Y. If not circle, U.

8. If the trumpet is a woodwind instrument, circle Z. If not, circle C.

9. If Charles Dickens wrote *David Copperfield*, circle T. If not, circle W.

10. If a telescope is used to view things far away, circle K. If not, circle M.

11. If the Statue of Liberty is located in Washington, D.C., circle E. If not, circle I.

Proverbial Codes

Use the code in the box to crack the code below and finish the sentences.

Letter	m	n	o	p	q	r	s	t	u	v	w	x	y
Code	A	B	C	D	E	F	G	H	I	J	K	L	M

Letter	z	a	b	c	d	e	f	g	h	i	j	k	l
Code	N	O	P	Q	R	S	T	U	V	W	X	Y	Z

1. Don't (oagzf) _____ your (otuowqze) _____ before
   they (tmfot) _____.

2. Birds of a (rqmftqd) _____ flock (fasqftqd) _____.

3. A (efufot) _____ in (fuyq) _____ saves
   (zuzq) _____.

4. A (bqzzk) _____ saved is a (bqzzk)_____
   (qmdzqp) _____.

5. Two (idazse)_____ don't make a (dustf) _____.

6. Where there is a (iuxx) _____, there is a (imk) _____.

7. (efduwq) _____ while the (udaz) _____ is hot.

8. A (imfotqp) _____ pot never (nauxe) _____.

More Proverbial Codes

Use this code to decode and finish the sentences.

Number	6	7	8	9	0	1	2	3	4	5	16	17	18
Code	A	B	C	D	E	F	G	H	I	J	K	L	M

Number	19	20	21	22	23	24	25	26	27	28	29	30	31
Code	N	O	P	Q	R	S	T	U	V	W	X	Y	Z

1. (17 20 20 16) _____ before you (17 0 6 21) _____.

2. Never put off until (25 20 18 20 23 23 20 28) _____ what
   can be done (25 20 9 6 30) _____.

3. A (1 23 4 0 19 9) _____ in (19 0 0 9) _____
   is a (1 23 4 0 19 9) _____ (4 19 9 0 0 9) _____.

4. The early (7 4 23 9) _____ catches the (28 20 23 18) _____.

5. All that (2 17 4 25 25 0 23 24) _____ is not (2 20 17 9) _____.

6. Don't (8 23 30) _____ over (24 21 4 17 17 0 9) _____ milk.

7. You never (16 19 20 28) _____ what you can do, (26 19 25 4 17)
   _____ you (25 23 30) _____.

8. Make (30 20 26 23 24 0 17 1) _____ necessary to (24 20 18 0 20 19 0)
   _____.

Communicating in Code

Different kinds of languages and codes have also been created to help people who can't see or hear well to communicate. Here is what the Braille alphabet would look like if it were printed in black and white instead of raised dots on a page which a blind person would read by touch.

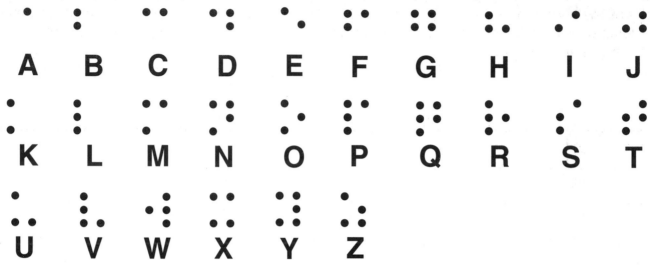

If you couldn't speak or hear, you would still be able to read, but how would you talk to your friends or family? One way would be to use your hands. Here is the Sign Language Manual Alphabet.

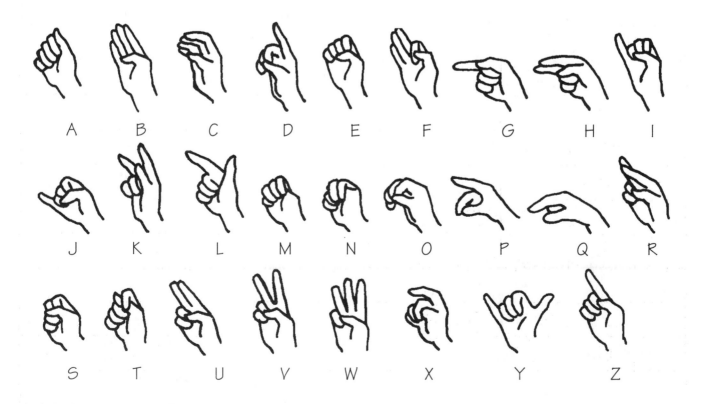

© Teacher Created Materials, Inc.

Communicating in Code *(cont.)*

Using one of the codes on the previous page, Morse code (page 184), or a code that you make up, write a paragraph about yourself. Include things like where you were born, how many brothers or sisters you have, your favorite subject, food, sport, etc. Use the space below to create your code. The symbols you use can be art or geometric forms, numbers, letters, dots and dashes, or any combination. If you create your own code, be sure to staple a copy of the code to the back of your paragraph. Place your coded paragraph in a file so other students can try to decode it. Be sure to try your hand at decoding the paragraphs written by other students.

My Code

A		S	
B		T	
C		U	
D		V	
E		W	
F		X	
G		Y	
H		Z	
I		1	
J		2	
K		3	
L		4	
M		5	
N		6	
O		7	
P		8	
Q		9	
R		10	

What Does This Mean?

Choose three of the words below. Take three sheets of paper and write one of the words at the bottom of each page. Draw an illustration or diagram to indicate what you think the wacky word might mean. Then, look up the wacky word. Once you understand the meaning, write, in your own words, a definition for the word on the back of your drawing. Post your Wacky Words art in the learning center or on a bulletin board chosen by your teacher for a Wacky Words Art Show. Leave the bottoms of your pages free so that your classmates can lift the pages and see what the words really mean.

abecedarian	**mellifluous**
agglomerate	**obstreperous**
agoraphobia	**piliferous**
alopecia	**isthmus**
aperture	**sigillography**
conundrum	**tessellate**
expurgate	**ululate**
hirsute	**ungulate**
lacuna	**verboten**

Rhyming Word Pairs

Find an adjective that rhymes with a noun so that together the two words have about the same meaning as the phrase that is given. An example has been done for you.

Example: A soaked dog = soggy doggy

1. a friend who does not arrive on time _____

2. an overweight rodent _____

3. a naughty boy _____

4. a crude guy _____

5. a beetle's cup _____

6. a lengthy tune _____

7. an plump weight feline _____

8. twice as much bother _____

9. a large hog _____

10. a girl from Switzerland _____

11. a skinny horse _____

12. a 100-watt bulb _____

13. a comical rabbit _____

14. a happy boy _____

15. a loafing flower _____

16. an unhappy father _____

17. a home for a rodent _____

18. without money _____

19. an irritated employer _____

20. fake coins _____

More Rhyming Word Pairs

Find an adjective that rhymes with a noun so that the two words together have about the same meaning as the phrase that is given. An example has been done for you.

Example: girl from Switzerland = Swiss miss

1. ailing William _____

2. mischievous boy _____

3. unhappy friend _____

4. bashful insect _____

5. fiesty primate _____

6. overweight referee _____

7. soft young dog _____

8. unhappy father _____

9. soaked dog _____

10. watered-down red juice _____

11. reliable Theodore _____

12. flower that is messy _____

13. tiny bug _____

14. ill hen _____

15. smart instrument _____

Palindromes

Palindromes are words, phrases, sentences, or numbers that read the same forward and backward. Write a palindrome that relates to each word or phrase below. An example has been done for you.

Example: Trick or joke = gag

1. midday _____

2. past tense of the verb do _____

3. a female sheep _____

4. robert's nickname _____

5. a small child _____

6. a little chick's noise _____

7. an organ of the body used for sight _____

8. a father's nickname _____

9. something that fails to work _____

10. the sound of a horn _____

11. something a baby wears _____

12. songs sung alone _____

13. a mother's nickname _____

14. an Eskimo canoe _____

15. even, flat _____

16. soda _____

17. a woman's name _____

18. a small dog _____

19. a brave or skillful act _____

20. relating to government or citizenship _____

Palindrome Word Find

Palindromes are words, phrases, sentences, or numbers that read the same forward and backward. Two examples are *121* and *Anna.* See how many palindromes you can find in this puzzle. (There are 35 words in all.)

```
S  J  B  L  A  D  B  B  U  O  F  M  B  E  W  E  Z  C
L  O  P  E  A  C  O  I  D  L  N  U  N  T  R  H  N  H
E  C  O  E  C  B  Q  O  B  J  T  M  M  O  E  A  B  T
V  T  M  Y  E  P  D  K  P  K  N  L  T  A  O  N  P  B
E  O  O  L  Z  P  M  H  E  V  E  I  Q  D  D  N  E  A
L  O  W  T  U  X  N  A  T  S  Q  M  T  H  I  A  E  T
A  T  J  P  S  R  N  U  Y  Z  K  A  R  S  T  H  M  X
N  A  D  D  B  D  R  R  Z  P  L  J  O  O  U  Q  O  J
J  Z  S  O  Z  I  A  T  K  W  O  H  A  L  T  R  X  O
D  E  E  D  M  G  D  A  B  S  S  P  W  O  C  O  L  T
B  Y  A  O  A  M  A  G  K  V  A  L  P  S  I  K  R  T
T  E  R  A  N  S  R  G  W  D  G  Z  F  R  V  G  V  O
E  A  R  K  N  L  S  L  O  I  A  L  U  P  I  K  M  O
R  E  P  A  P  E  R  U  W  D  S  N  I  O  C  M  O  T
R  K  H  Y  S  X  P  S  N  J  E  O  N  T  E  R  M  G
E  O  K  A  F  O  I  U  D  U  D  M  B  A  C  E  B  I
T  H  A  K  D  J  M  N  X  R  G  H  E  W  C  A  B  T
S  E  E  S  U  N  X  W  O  A  L  S  K  A  G  Z  P  O
```

Match That Author!

Cut out the cards below and place them facedown. Play by yourself or with one or two others. Turn over two cards. If a work of literature and its author match, keep the cards and play again. If you don't have a match, turn them back over and try again, or if playing with others, give up your turn.

Titles

Little Women	**Anne of Green Gables**
A Wrinkle in Time	**The Outsiders**
Tom Sawyer	**Watership Down**
Bridge to Terabithia	**Jane Eyre**
Little House on the Prairie	**Island of the Blue Dolphins**

Match That Author! *(cont.)*

Authors

Louisa May Alcott	Lucy Maud Montgomery
Madeleine L'Engle	S. E. Hinton
Mark Twain	Richard Adams
Katherine Paterson	Charlotte Brontë
Laura Ingalls Wilder	Scott O'Dell

Crazy, Mixed-Up Sentences

Follow the directions on pages 197–199 to make this writing activity. To make the Subject Cards, reproduce this page on red cardstock or sturdy paper or glue it onto red construction paper. Cut apart the cards. Then make the Verb Cards (on page 198) and the Complement Cards (page 199).

Subject Cards

My teacher	A big green monster	My grandmother	A little baby
An alien from Mars	A koala bear	A humpback whale	A slimy creature
A dog as big as a horse	An orange grasshopper	A cute little boy	The trash collector
A hairy caterpillar	A large, blue refrigerator	A rock star	A giant raccoon

Crazy, Mixed-Up Sentences *(cont.)*

To make the Verb Cards, reproduce this page on blue cardstock or sturdy paper or glue it onto blue construction paper. Cut out the cards. Then make the Complement Cards (page 199).

Verb Cards

leaps	growls	roars	giggles
sits	slithers	swims	sings
rolls	crawls	flies	eats
snores	cries	somersaults	slips

Crazy, Mixed-Up Sentences *(cont.)*

To make the Complement Cards, reproduce this page on orange cardstock or sturdy paper, or glue it onto orange construction paper. Cut out the cards. Then have students, in the learning center, mix up the cards and choose one of each color. They will write the sentence that is created from the draw of one card of each color.

Example: A giant raccoon somersaults in a large vat of peanut butter.

Complement Cards

on my head.	around the world.	in a large vat of peanut butter.	with my dad.
in the forest.	at the airport.	behind the garage.	under the car.
all the time.	at our house.	in the bathtub.	in the air.
through the forest.	on top of a mountain.	in the classroom.	on a piece of paper.

Economics Game

This game has thirty economics terms that players must match with definitions.

Materials

- card stock of any color to print game cards and to mount rules and answer key
- laminating materials

Construction

1. Print the game cards on colored card stock. Laminate the pages, then cut out the cards.
2. Trim the rules box and the answer key on page 303. Mount on card stock of the same color as used for the game cards. Laminate them.

Rules for "Economics Vocabulary"

This game is for three or four players and one judge. Pencil and paper are needed for keeping score.

1. Judge shuffles cards and deals seven cards to each player. Stack remaining cards face down. Turn first card faceup and place to one side to start discard pile.

2. Player to the left of the dealer goes first. Play moves to the left.

3. Begin each turn by drawing one card from either the facedown or faceup deck. Player makes any possible matches between vocabulary word cards and definition cards.

4. A matching pair is laid faceup on the table for all to see. Any player may challenge a match. Judge checks answer key according to card number.

5. If match is incorrect, player must return incorrect match to cards in hand, take two additional cards from facedown deck, and discard one card to end turn.

6. If match is correct, any player who challenged the match must take two cards from the facedown deck. Player with correct match lays that match aside and makes any other possible matches before ending his or her turn by discarding.

7. When one player is out of cards, play stops. Points are recorded. Each match is worth five points.

8. Shuffle and deal to play another round. When game time is over, the player with the most points is the winner.

Economics Game *(cont.)*

1. items such as land, buildings, tools, money, etc., that are used in the production of other goods $	**CAPITAL RESOURCES** $
2. someone who uses goods or services $	**CONSUMER** $
3. the study of the manufacture, distribution, sale, and use of goods and services $	**ECONOMICS** $
4. how much in the way of goods and services people want and are able and willing to buy at a given price $	**DEMAND** $
5. materials that are produced for people to buy or things that can be seen and touched $	**GOODS** $

Economics Game *(cont.)*

6. jobs that people do for other people in return for pay $	**SERVICES** $
7. things in nature for which man has found use $	**NATURAL RESOURCES** $
8. the amount of money that a company makes after all the costs of running the business have been paid $	**PROFIT** $
9. the amount of money that must be spent to get a certain good or services $	**COST** $
10. a person who makes goods or provides services $	**PRODUCER** $

Economics Game *(cont.)*

11. the amount of a product that is available for people to purchase $	**SUPPLY** $
12. things that people would like to have but can live without, such as TVs $	**WANTS** $
13. things that people must have in order to survive, such as food $	**NEEDS** $
14. the things you give up when making a choice between two things $	**OPPORTUNITY COST** $
15. making and providing goods and services for people to buy $	**PRODUCTION** $

Economics Game *(cont.)*

16. people with skills who do a job $	**HUMAN RESOURCES** $
17. money paid to someone in exchange for the use of that person's property $	**RENT** $
18. money that is paid to a worker for the amount of time that has been worked $	**WAGES OR SALARY** $
19. when there are not enough goods and services to satisfy the wants and needs of the people $	**SCARCITY** $
20. a business owner $	**ENTREPRENEUR** $

Economics Game *(cont.)*

21. the person who hires someone else to do work $	**EMPLOYER** $
22. a person who is hired by someone else to do a job $	**EMPLOYEE** $
23. when people do the jobs that they are interested in and do best $	**SPECIALIZATION** $
24. money that is paid on a loan by the borrower for the use of that money $	**INTEREST** $
25. a general rise in the price level of goods and services $	**INFLATION** $

Economics Game (cont.)

26. times when people are out of work and businesses are doing badly $	**RECESSION** $
27. shares of a business that can be bought and sold $	**STOCK** $
28. someone who puts money into a business hoping to make a profit $	**INVESTOR** $
29. a contest between businesses or people to get the most customers or the best price $	**COMPETITION** $
30. different jobs needed in production which are divided among various workers $	**DIVISION OF LABOR** $

Color This Design

Color this design so that no shapes of the same color touch one another. You may use only three colors. (**Hint:** Think about the design before you begin to color.)

I've Been Framed!

Each number in the boxes below is written within a different shape or frame. Using this as a guide, write the correct number in each shape below and solve each problem.

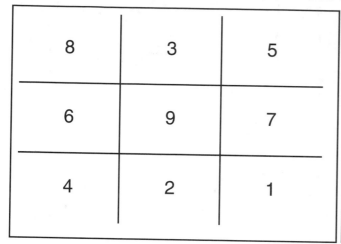

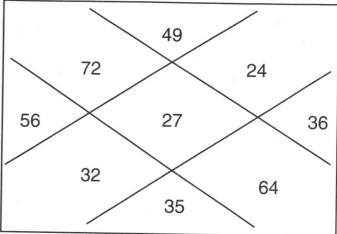

1. $(\wedge \div \llcorner) \times (\diamondsuit \div \sqcup) = $ _____

2. $(\langle\rangle \div \urcorner) \times (\vee \div \square) = $ _____

3. $(\vee \div \square) \times (\langle \div \lrcorner) = $ _____

4. $(> \div \square) \times (\sqcap \div \lrcorner) = $ _____

5. $(< \div \rceil) \times (\wedge \div \square) = $ _____

Hidden Meanings

Explain the meaning of each box.

F ꟻ A A C Ɔ E Ǝ	man ――― board	LE VEL
1. _____	2. _____	3. _____
wear ――― long	d d e e r e r	HEAD ――― HEELS
4. _____	5. _____	6. _____
businesspleasure	coORDERurt	N W O T
7. _____	8. _____	9. _____
Ban ana	O ――― B.S. M.A. Ph.D.	sota
10. _____	11. _____	12. _____

More Hidden Meanings

Explain the meaning of each box.

B R A I N E D	**GROUND** FT FT FT FT FT FT	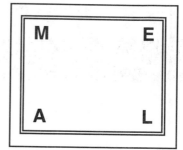
1. _____	2. _____	3. _____
knee light	League	**Man** Campus
4. _____	5. _____	6. _____
NEpainCK	**Check**	Tim
7. _____	8. _____	9. _____
Once ——— Lightly	**your hat keep it**	School
10. _____	11. _____	12. _____

Word Chains

To make a word chain, each new word must begin with the last letter of the previous word. For example, if the category is Famous Americans, a possible word chain would be the following: George Bush—Herbert Hoover—Ronald Reagan, etc. This can be adapted to any area of study or played in teams, each team taking turns adding to the chain.

Countries	Proper Nouns	Foods
Chile	Betsy Ross	hot dog
England	Salt Lake City	green bean

Math Squares

Cut out the boxes below. Arrange them so that each touching edge has the same answer.

21 · 33 · 9 x 5	2 x 22 · 76 · 16 x 2	5 x 5 · 60 ÷ 5 · 4 x 8	45 · 4 x 19
3 x 4 · 16 · 3 x 5 · 4 x 8	32 · 49 ÷ 7 · 42 · 12	15 · 9 x 9 · 4 x 16	3 x 11 · 44 · 6 x 10 · 7
7 x 9 · 64	4 x 5 · 7 x 8 · 3 x 6	28 · 5 x 12 · 56 · 4 x 4	2 x 10 · 63 · 2 x 6
54 · 7 x 4 · 3 x 7	9 x 6 · 18	6 x 7 · 36 ÷ 2 · 4 x 9	3 x 6 · 50 ÷ 2

Factors and Multiples

This is a game for two players. Using the numbers below, the first player marks an O on a multiple—for example, 15. The next player marks an X on each of the factors of that multiple. In this example, the second player would mark an X on 1, 3, 5, and 15.

Then the second player marks a new multiple with X, and the first player marks Os on all the unmarked multiples of that number. A player may not mark a number that is marked already.

A player may only mark a multiple that still has some factors remaining for the opponent to mark.

When there are no multiples left that have factors to mark, the game is over. Total the number of Xs and Os. The player with the most numbers marked is the winner of the round.

1	7	13	19	25
2	8	14	20	26
3	9	15	21	27
4	10	16	22	28
5	11	17	23	29
6	12	18	24	30

Improper Fraction Mix-Up

The top boxes contain improper fractions, and the bottom ones contain mixed numbers. For each improper fraction, find its mixed number in the bottom boxes. Then write the word from the improper fraction box into the correct mixed number box.

3/2 **to**	7/4 **any**	10/8 **It**	16/12 **than**	11/7 **have**	15/9 **interesting**
16/10 **read**	19/11 **never**	24/10 **better**	14/12 **have**	22/13 **is**	21/15 **to**
13/9 **very**	16/14 **books**	22/18 **read**	18/10 **all.**	33/24 **some**	33/18 **at**
1 1/4	1 9/13	2 2/5	1 2/5	1 4/7	1 3/5
1 3/8	1 4/9	1 2/3	1 1/7	1 1/3	1 8/11
1 1/2	1 1/6	1 2/9	1 3/4	1 5/6	1 4/5

Fractured Fractions

This is a game for two players. The object of the game is to make two fractions and find their sum. Whoever has the greater sum is the winner.

Use index cards or regular playing cards to make two sets of the numbers 1 through 6. If using playing cards, have the aces represent the 1's.

Shuffle the cards, and place them facedown. Player one draws the top three cards and chooses two to write a proper fraction on his or her sheet. Then player two repeats the process. This continues until both players have each drawn six cards and written two proper fractions on their game sheets. Both players should then find the sum of both fractions. If they disagree about the sum, they should work the problems together until they agree on the correct answer. The player with the greater sum is the winner. Be sure to change improper fractions to mixed numbers.

Player One Game Sheet   **Player Two Game Sheet**

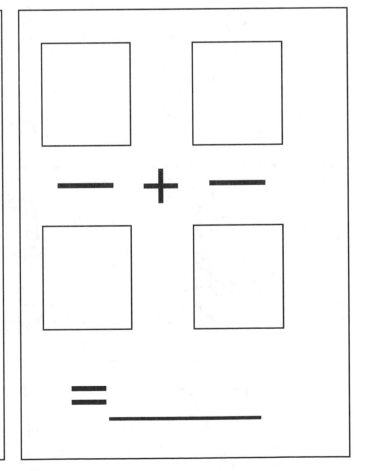

Close the Box

This is a game for two players. Use the game board below, two dice, and nine counters such as beans, coins, small pebbles, etc. The object of the game is to have the lowest score possible. The first player to reach 45 points is out.

To play the game, the first player rolls the dice. He or she can either cover both numbers shown or add them up and cover one number. For example, if a three and a four are rolled, the player can either cover the three and the four or just the seven. The same player continues rolling until he or she rolls a number that cannot be used. At that time, the remaining numbers are added up. If the sum is six or less, the player may discard one die and continue rolling the other one until he or she rolls a number that cannot be used. At that time, the sum of the remaining numbers is recorded as the player's score. If all of the numbers have been covered, the player earns 0 points. The board is then cleared, and it becomes the next player's turn. Play continues until one player has not reached 45 points. That player is the winner.

1	2	3
4	5	6
7	8	9

Decimal Derby

This is a game for two players. The object of the game is to make two numbers and find their product. Whoever has the greater number is the winner.

Use index cards or regular playing cards to make the numbers 0 through 9. If using playing cards, have a face card represents 0 and an ace represents 1.

Shuffle the cards and place them facedown. Player one draws the top card and writes the number somewhere on his or her sheet. Then player two repeats the process. This continues until both players have drawn four cards and written the numbers on their game sheets. Once a number has been written on the sheet, it cannot be changed. Both players should then find the products of both numbers. If they disagree about the product, a calculator may be used to determine the correct answer. The player with the greater product is the winner.

Player One Game Sheet

Player Two Game Sheet

Spaceship Flip

This game will help students in geometry who are working on flips, slides, and turns. Any students who are fans of the video game *Tetris* will enjoy this game. The object of the game is to color more of the spaceship than your opponent does. Have the students work in groups of two. Each student should have a copy of the spaceship on page 219, a set of the shapes below (cut out), and a crayon or marker to color the squares.

To prepare for the game, students should make a spinner by placing a pencil or pen with a paper clip around it in the middle of the circle below.

The first player spins the spinner to determine which shape to color on his or her spaceship. Students may use the cutout shapes to help them visualize how the shape would look if turned or flipped. Once a player determines which squares of the spaceship to choose, he or she should color in those squares. The next player repeats the process. If a player spins on a shape that he or she cannot fill in, then he or she is out. The game is over when both players are out. The player who colors more of the spaceship is the winner.

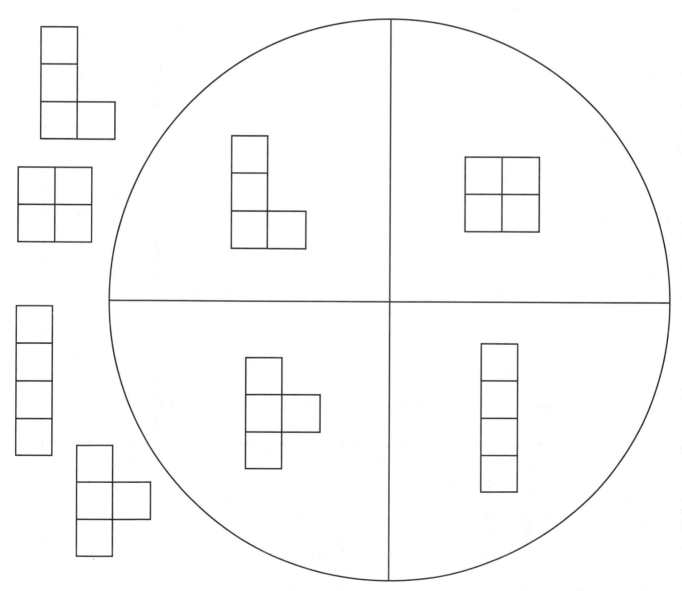

Spaceship Flip (cont.)

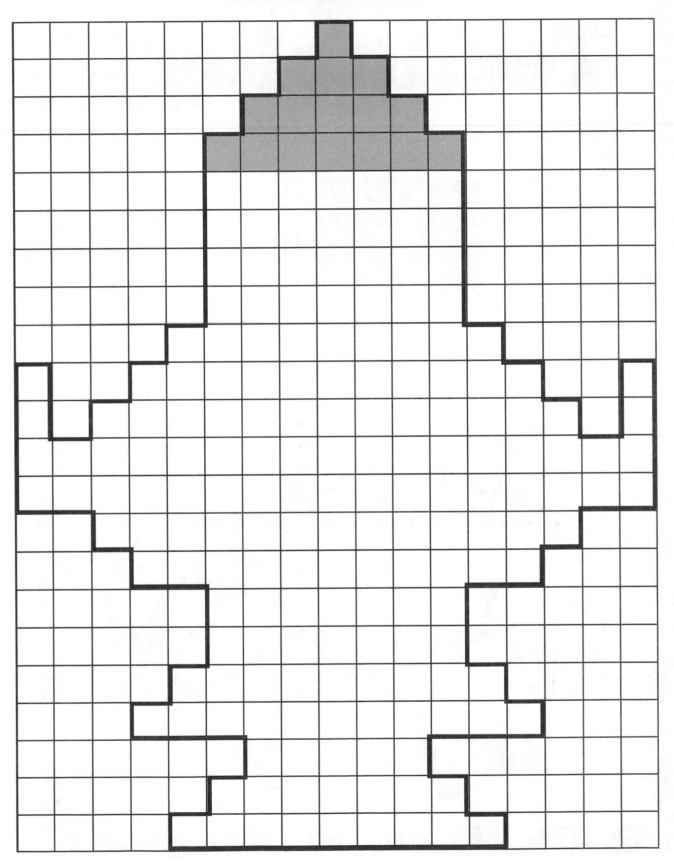

Technology

Utilizing the Internet

As technology is integrated into the classroom, instruction is moving toward a constructive approach in which students become involved in real-world situations that require the development of problem-solving skills. Students are no longer limited to the resources in their classroom, school, or district. They learn how to solve problems using up-to-date information that is available through online sources. In many instances, this work is done in a cooperative learning environment. The teacher's role becomes one of facilitator and guide.

Be sure to give yourself enough time to feel comfortable with the materials in this book and the World Wide Web environment before you do an activity or start an online project with your students.

The Internet is a good place for:

- locating information not available in textbooks or the classroom/school library.

- finding and contacting experts in a particular subject area.

- utilizing government information or that which is not accessible to the general public.

- sharing information with other teachers and/or students from anywhere in the world.*

- publishing students' work online.

- obtaining timely information (breaking news).

- reducing professional isolation by helping teachers keep in contact with professional colleagues worldwide.

- helping students retain material.

- gaining maximum educational value with limited time commitment.

The Internet is not a good place to:

- find summaries or quick overviews of a topic.

- replace hands-on activities such as drawing, writing, building, etc., although it can supplement these activities.

- have active face-to-face interaction with other students and teachers.

---

* If you would like specific lessons for teaching students how to send E-mail messages, see *Internet Activities for Social Studies* (Teacher Created Materials #2405).

Internet Safety Rules for Students

1. **I will not give out personal information** such as my address, telephone number, parents' work number or address, or the name and location of my school without my parents' permission.

2. **I will tell my parents right away** if I come across any information that makes me feel uncomfortable.

3. **I will never agree to get together with someone I "meet" online** without first checking with my parents. If my parents agree to the meeting, I will be sure that it is in a public place and will bring my mother or father along.

4. **I will never send a person my picture** or anything else without first checking with my parents.

5. **I will not respond to any negative messages** that are mean or in any way make me feel uncomfortable. It is not my fault if I get a message like that. If I do, I will tell my parents right away so they can contact the online service.

6. **I will talk with my parents so that we can set up rules for going online.** We will decide upon the time of day I can be online, the length of time I can be online, and the appropriate areas for me to visit. I will not access other areas or break the rules without their permission.

Plan for Instruction

As with any instructional experience, successful use of the Internet and World Wide Web in the classroom involves advance planning. This planning is not much different from the planning teachers ordinarily do for their regular classroom activities/lessons. Remember that planning is an ongoing process, and you will need to plan for both long-term and short-term goals. The following list of suggestions can help you plan more effectively.

Planning Suggestions

1. Know why you are planning to use the Internet or World Wide Web. Have a written plan posted in your room.

2. Prepare your students in advance so they have a clear understanding of what you want them to accomplish as part of this experience. Explain your goals and objectives to them.

3. Check out the sites you want to access in advance so you have a reasonable assurance that these sites will be available at the times students will be looking for information.

4. Prepare for expected and unexpected outcomes. Have alternate sites ready which contain essentially the same information as your first choice so you can send students to the alternate site if the first sites are unavailable.

5. Allow students enough freedom to pursue other links they may find during their "surfing." Monitor their activities to be sure they stay "on task" as much as possible, but allow them to follow some of their own choices. If they choose to go off on a tangent, have them make note of it and explain what they expected to gain from following that strand instead of the one that was assigned. Sometimes the best learning occurs when it is unintentional.

Create Your Own Advertisement!

Objectives

- Creating an attractive advertisement
- Enlarging font size
- Changing font style and color
- Accessing pictures from a CD-ROM
- Understanding correct proportions for a document

> **Middlebury Middle School**
> Used Book Drive Oct 1-5
> **Bring your used books to the school library.**

Program Needed

Use a drawing program that is very flexible but also can make professional looking documents such as *AppleWorks® (ClarisWorks)* or *Microsoft Publisher®.*

Instructions

1. Students will be creating advertisements for a particular event at school, such as a musical or collecting canned food for a food drive. Assign students a topic and provide for them the who, what, where, and when facts.

2. Show students effective advertisements in a newspaper and compare those to poor advertisements.

3. Students will then construct their slogans or advertisements, remembering to include the important details. (Words should be highly visible and easy to read.)

4. Students may want to add a border or create their own.

5. Students should add appropriate clip art, probably from a CD-ROM. (This would be a good time to explain to students how to access the perfect picture from a CD-ROM.)

6. Finally, proof work and print.

Extension Ideas

A teacher could run a contest for the best advertisement, which would be voted on by students or faculty members. Also, a teacher could post a list of posters or advertisements which need to be made for other teachers or the administration. Students could earn community service hours upon completion of a project. Students could also create posters depicting the main characters from a novel read in class.

Writing Good Descriptions

A good written description should reflect the real world. The activity given at the Web site shown below involves creating a character for a story.

Objective: Students learn how to write good descriptions for characters.

Materials: Describing Physical Characteristics (page 226)

            Describing Personality Traits (page 227)

Primary Web Site: Educational Courseware: Writing
            http://www.crl.com/~boeschen/Nfoshare/Write/i_see_it.htm

Background Knowledge: Ask students to use some of the information they learned about folk tale characters to create their own characters. The directions for this activity say that students may use some of their classmates' traits in the character descriptions they write. As a result, you may need to remind students to be sensitive to the feelings of others when using the traits of real people.

Teaching the Lesson

1. Have students begin by discussing how they could describe a character in a story. Ask them to tell what things would be important to know about that character. Lead students to conclude which physical characteristics and personality traits should be described.

2. Ask students to complete Describing Physical Characteristics (page 226) to decide what is important about the character's appearance.

3. Have students complete Describing Personality Traits (page 227) to decide what is important about the character's personality.

4. Invite students to share their idea webs with the class. If you prefer, you may wish to display these on two separate bulletin boards, one for physical characteristics and the other for personality traits.

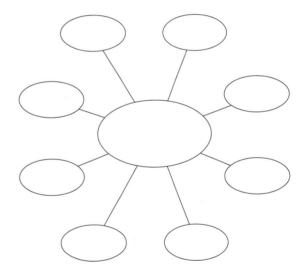

Extended Activities

1. Have students use their idea webs to write a story about the characters they described.

2. Invite students to draw and fill in idea webs to describe the physical characteristics and personality traits of their favorite television characters.

3. Ask students to choose their favorite storybook characters. Have them draw and fill in idea webs to describe the physical characteristics and personality traits of these characters.

Describing Physical Characteristics

Primary Web Site: Educational Courseware: Writing
http://www.crl.com/~boeschen/Nfoshare/Write/i_see_it.htm

Think about what you want your character to look like. Describe the physical characteristics of your character. Use the idea web to organize your information.

Physical Characteristics

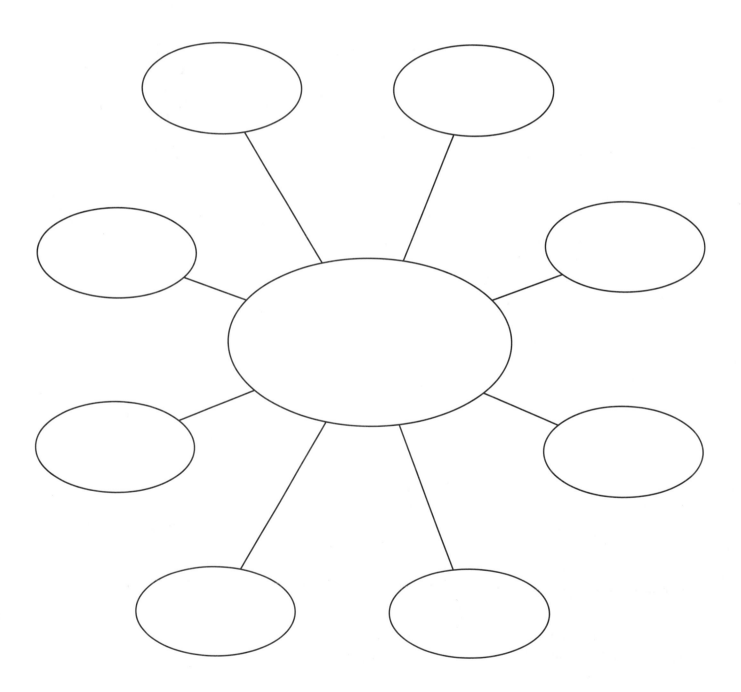

Describing Personality Traits

Primary Web Site: Educational Courseware: Writing
http://www.crl.com/~boeschen/Nfoshare/Write/i_see_it.htm

Think about how your character behaves. Describe your character's personality traits. Use the idea web to organize your information.

Personality Traits

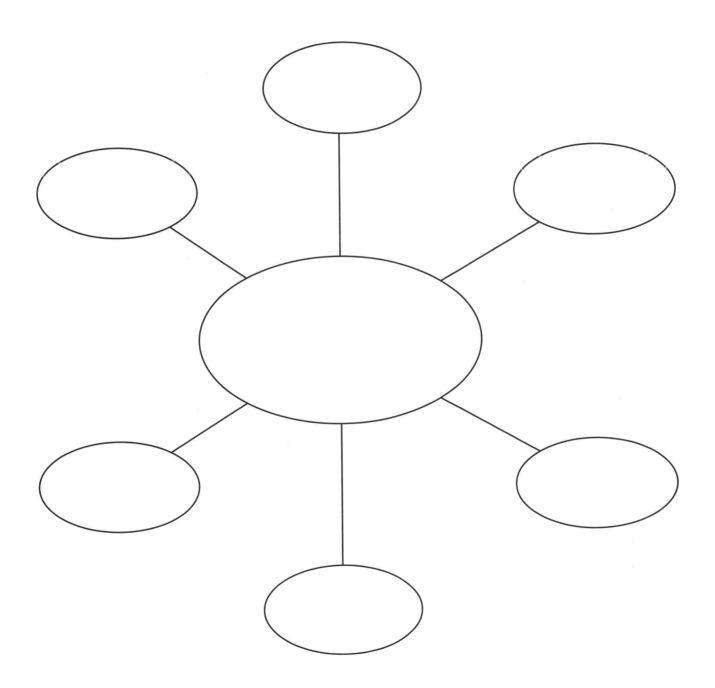

Computer Poetry

Objectives

- Understanding different types of poetry such as haiku, tanka, cinquain, and limerick
- Counting syllables in words correctly
- Typing extemporaneously
- Centering and underlining titles
- Accessing clip art from a CD-ROM
- Spell checking documents

Program Needed

Use a word-processing program such as *Microsoft Word®* or *AppleWorks (ClarisWorks)*. Have clip art accessible from a CD-ROM.

Instructions

1. Discuss with students different formats for poetry, such as haiku, tanka, cinquain, and limerick. Explain to the students about counting the syllables. Show them an example of each type of format on the next few pages. (The students can pick one poem to do or make a poetry booklet containing many forms of poetry.)

2. Students will choose their poems and begin typing titles. Demonstrate how to center and underline the title.

3. Students will begin typing the bodies of their poems extemporaneously, keeping in mind the syllable and line structure.

4. Put students in pairs to check one another's poems for content and form.

5. Students can then find appropriate pictures to illustrate their poems from a CD-ROM or the Internet.

6. Each student's work should be spell checked and printed.

Extension Ideas

Poetry books make nice gifts for a parent or grandparent. Consider having each student choose a theme for his or her poetry book. Students may want to post some of their best poetry on the Internet or on the school Web site. Consider pairing your students with younger students to teach the basics of how to write a poem.

Haiku Poem

Bustling Bees

The bees are busy
Finding petals to land on
So they can get food.

Haiku format

Haiku is a form of unrhymed poetry that had its beginning in Japan. Haiku poetry usually describes something about nature or the seasons. Each poem is three lines, and the number of syllables in each line follows this pattern:

Line 1: five syllables

Line 2: seven syllables

Line 3: five syllables

Tanka Poem

Icicles on the Trees

The pine trees are tall
Covered with snowflakes and ice
Swaying in the wind
Soon it will all sadly melt
But it was a sight to see.

Tanka format

According to Asian tradition, if someone writes you a haiku, you are to write a tanka poem to them in return. It is a way of saying thank you. The tanka poem does not have to be on the same subject. A tanka is five lines long and the number of syllables in each line follows this pattern:

Line 1: five syllables

Line 2: seven syllables

Line 3: five syllables

Line 4: seven syllables

Line 5: seven syllables

Cinquain Poem

Flowers
Colorful petals
Fill the air with fragrance
Good food for bees and butterflies
Beauty

Cinquain format

A cinquain is a simple, five-line verse which follows this form:

Line 1:   one noun of two syllables (the subject of the poem)

Line 2:   four to five syllables (words that describe the subject of the poem)

Line 3:   six syllables (telling an action of the subject)

Line 4:   eight syllables (expressing a feeling or sharing information about the subject)

Line 5:   another two-syllable noun describing the subject

Limerick Poem

There once was a boy from Delray

Who was light as a feather they say

The wind came along

And blew very strong

And carried the poor boy away.

Limerick format

A limerick is a short, silly poem. Most limericks are five lines long following these rules:

Lines 1, 2, and 5 rhyme

Lines 1, 2, and 5 have either eight, nine, or ten syllables

Lines 3 and 4 rhyme

Lines 3 and 4 have either five, six, or seven syllables

Properties of Matter

If you are interested in something, it is always nice to find a brochure that tells you all about it. In this activity, the children can make their own brochure about the stages of matter.

Grade Level: three

Duration: about 30 minutes computer time

Materials: brochure paper or plain paper, a word-processing program, a teacher-made identification work sheet

Procedure: The students will make a brochure advertising the stages of matter.

Before the Computer

- Students try to identify as many solids, liquids, and gases as they can at home and at school. They can bring samples to school, and the class can discuss each one to see into which category it fits.

    Solid: stays the same shape, stays the same size, can be touched, can be seen

    Liquid: flows, changes shape, may or may not be seen

    Gas: changes shape, very low density, cannot be seen, cannot be felt

- Each student fills out a work sheet and then the class can consolidate the lists.

- Determine a definition for matter and one each for liquid, solid, and gas.

- Compose a paragraph telling about the activity and what tests were used to determine the stages of the different objects.

On the Computer

- Use a program that has special fold capabilities for brochures, such as *Microsoft Publisher*®, *Press Writer*®, *Printmaster Gold 3.0*®, or you can use your regular word processor, such as *Microsoft Word*, *Microsoft Works*®, or *AppleWorks (ClarisWorks)*. If your word processor doesn't have special formatting for brochures, just go into page setup and change to landscape orientation and three columns. It will work fine.

- Determine what will go on each fold. The title and a paragraph describing the activity should go on the fold that will be the front.

- On each of the inside folds, make a list of objects that fit into the stages of matter: solid, liquid and gas—one per fold.

- On another fold you might want to list objects that can be made to go from one stage to another, such as water, cheese, and metal.

Extension Activities

- Besides classifying the objects as solid, liquid, or gas, the students could expand the list of objects whose states can change to include information about reversing the change. It is easy to re-freeze water after it has thawed, but after it has changed into a gas, how easily can you change it back?

Properties of Matter *(cont.)*

Extension Activities *(cont.)*

- Determine which objects have odors.
- Determine which objects conduct heat or cold.
- Determine if an object can be in two stages at once. Discuss colloids.

Internet Links

- *http://www.eecs.umich.edu/mathscience/funexperiments/agesubject/physicalsciences.html*
  Many physical science activities are sorted by levels: early elementary, later elementary, middle school, and high school.

- *http://192.239.146.18/resources/Science/PSAM.html*
  Downloadable activity files here include "Definition of Matter," "Measurement of Mass," and about 30 others.

States of Matter Work Sheet			
Object	Solid	Liquid	Gas

Properties of Matter *(cont.)*

Here is an example of a brochure that explains the properties of matter. The illustration on the right shows an example of the front cover of the brochure. The illustration below shows an example of the inside of the brochure.

Cover

Inside

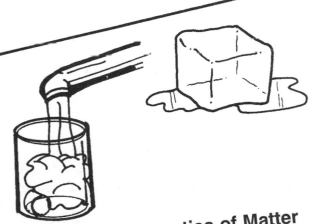

States and Properties of Matter

Matter is anything that has mass (weight) and takes up space. A property is something about matter that can be observed and indicates something about matter, such as its color, its smell, or its shape.

One of the properties of matter is its form of state. Three states of matter are liquid, solid, and gas. A *liquid* has a definite volume, but has no shape of its own. It changes its shape to fit the container it is in. A *solid* has a certain shape and volume of its own. A *gas* does not have a shape of its own or a certain volume. Many times you cannot even see gas.

Inside this brochure you will find many things listed by their state of matter.

Investigations done by Mrs. McMillin's 3rd Grade Class

Page 1   Page 2

Investigating Matter—Making Models

Learning why we use models and designing our own can help us realize the benefits of models and review what we know about atoms.

Grade Level: three to five

Duration: 15–30 minutes computer time

Materials

- a drawing program such as *Kid Pix*® or *Paint*®
- evaluation sheet (page 237)

Procedure: After studying atoms and discussing the importance of models, the students will design and draw their own models using the approach that seems clearest to them.

Before the Computer

- Study atoms.
- Examine models and discuss the purpose of using models.

On the Computer

- Research different kinds of atoms and their makeup. You may use the Internet. The site at *http://users.boone.net/yinon/default.html* is a good place to start. Using what they have learned about models and what they have learned about atoms, the students will design and produce a model of an atom.
- The students will choose what type of atom to model. (Oxygen, carbon, and sodium atoms are relatively easy, but some students will be more ambitious.)

Internet Links

- *http://www.tannerm.com/* (click on Atoms and Elements)
  Advanced information about atoms is found here.

- *http://pdg.lbl.gov/cpep/startstandard.html*
  This is an interesting presentation of the atom.

- *http://pdg.lbl.gov/cpep/adventure_home.html*
  This is the larger project within which the previous presentation of the atom is set. The whole project is worth viewing by the students.

Investigating Matter—Making Models *(cont.)*

Thinking Questions Before You Start

1. What does the word "model" mean?
2. What models have you seen?
3. Did these models help you understand the subject they represented?
4. Why do we make models?
5. Why would anyone want a model of an atom?
6. How can having a model of an atom help us?

Evaluating Models	Answers
1. What parts does this model have? Does it have enough parts? Does it have too many parts? Explain.	
2. How does this model represent the atom?	
3. How is this model very different from the atom?	
4. How could examining this model help us?	
5. How could examining this model give us a wrong idea?	
6. How could this model be improved?	
7. Why would the changes in question 6 make the model better?	

The Nine Planets

Objectives

- Locating Internet addresses on the computer
- Scanning through information to find facts
- Typing facts in boxes
- Copying and pasting appropriate clip art

Program Needed

You will need access to the Internet and a program in which you can paste clip art and draw boxes and lines. *Power Point®* or *AppleWorks (ClarisWorks)* will work well for this project.

Instructions

1. Students should launch the Internet and find the Nine Planets Web site at **http://www.seds.org/billa/tnp/**

2. Give students one planet to study. Students will be navigating through this Web site to find particular facts on their planets, such as distance from the sun, length of day, composition of the atmosphere, temperature, and the diameter.

3. Depending on the skill level and the time allotted, the teacher or students may make a template with seven boxes similar to the one on the shown in the example below.

4. Students will title these boxes "Average Distance from the Sun," "Temperature," etc. The last box should be pretty large and be entitled "Fun Facts."

5. Students will type their information. Once students have typed all of their information in a box, they may need to enlarge or shrink the box to fit all of their information comfortably. Students may also need to shrink the font if information still does not fit.

6. Students will then find appropriate pictures either from a CD-ROM or the Internet.

7. Student's work should be proofed, spell-checked, and then printed.

Extension Ideas

As a follow-up to this lesson, students may want to find one or two more Web sites about their planet. Students may want to expand the Fun Facts box onto another page to fit 6–10 other facts. Students could print two copies of the fact page. With the extra copy, students can cut each of their fun facts into strips. Students can deposit these facts into a bin. The teacher could pull out one fact, read it, and have students guess which planet it is.

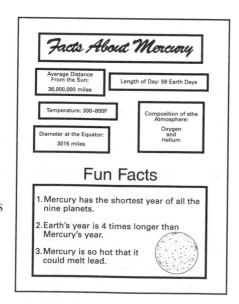

A Year in the Life of a Tree

There are two types of trees—evergreen and deciduous. The evergreen keeps its leaves (needles) all year long, and the deciduous tree lose its leaves in the autumn.

You are going to follow the life of a deciduous tree through one full school year, noting the changes in each season. You will be making a spring tree, summer tree, autumn tree, and winter tree. This activity is designed to be used with the drawing software *Kid Pix*. (For additional activities, see *Kid Pix Activity Kit: Seasons* by Teacher Created Materials.)

1. Select the Wacky Brush option and click on the down arrow at the bottom of the screen to reach the level where you find a tree.

2. Click on the tree option and the color brown.

3. Move your cursor to the middle part of the screen. Hold down the option key and click.

4. Start by adding some elements to your picture that show it is spring. To make leaves for your spring tree, click on the arrow to go to the level where the bubbles are shown. Click on the bubbles option and the color green. Put some leaves on your tree.

5. Use the Wacky Pencil tool to draw roots for your tree. This is optional.

6. To add grass, select the Wacky Brush tool and locate the grass option. Click on the grass option and green. Move your mouse horizontally across the screen, holding the mouse button down.

A Year in the Life of a Tree *(cont.)*

7. Select the Rubber Stamp tool and look through the options to find birds, flowers, animals, and people to add to your picture.

8. In *Kid Pix* select Type Text from the GOODIES menu. In *Kid Pix Studio*® select the Typewriter tool. Select a font from the bottom of the screen. Click on the screen and type in the word "Spring." Write a sentence about the effects of spring on a tree. Be sure to put your name on your picture.

9. Save and print your picture in the Itsy Bitsy size.

10. Modify the steps above and add your own variations to create your summer, fall, and winter trees.

What Else Can We Do: Now you are gong to make pictures that represent the other three seasons. After you print each of the four pictures, you will put them on a paper plate for display. Be sure to print each picture in Itsy Bitsy size.

1. To make your pictures into a display, use a paper plate as a base.

2. You can use the Electric Mixer tool and then choose the raindrop option on the far right to make snowflakes and/or rain.

3. You may want to print in large size to make a book of seasons.

4. To write a story about the tree passing through the year, choose a blank screen. Select Type Text from the GOODIES menu along with a large font for the title and then choose a smaller font for the story.

5. Save and print your story to accompany the pictures.

6. You can easily put your pictures into a slide show presentation. When you save your work, put each screen into a folder that you have labeled "Seasons." Open the SlideShow screen and place each picture into a moving van. You can record a story about each picture by selecting the sound button. You have 32 seconds in which to record.

7. You can make a poster about the year in the life of the tree that you observed. Describe different types of trees that are classified as deciduous and why you chose to observe the tree that you picked. What did you learn about the life of your deciduous tree?

8. You can make decorative cards with your Itsy Bitsy sized picture prints by gluing them on the front of a piece of colorful construction paper that you fold in half. Write a letter or short note inside and decorate.

A Year in the Life of a Tree *(cont.)*

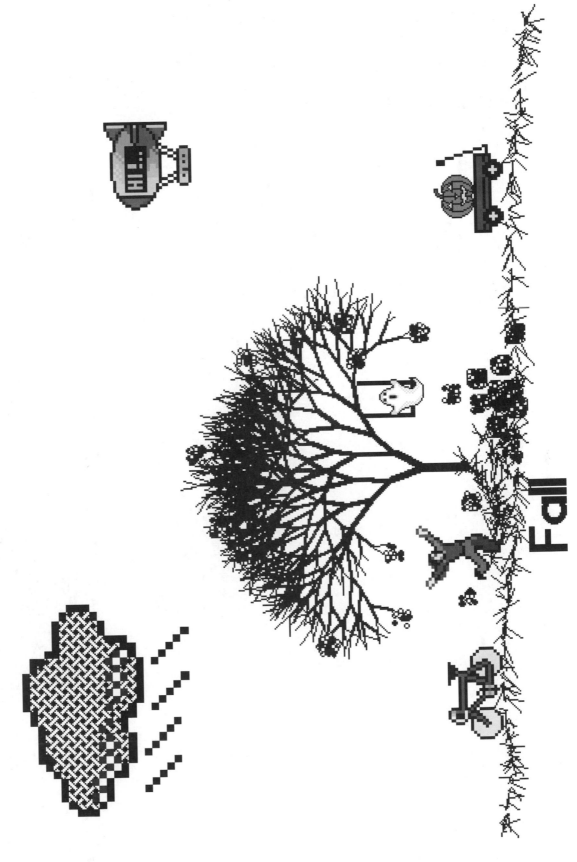

Fall

A Year in the Life of a Tree *(cont.)*

Winter

A Year in the Life of a Tree *(cont.)*

Spring

A Year in the Life of a Tree *(cont.)*

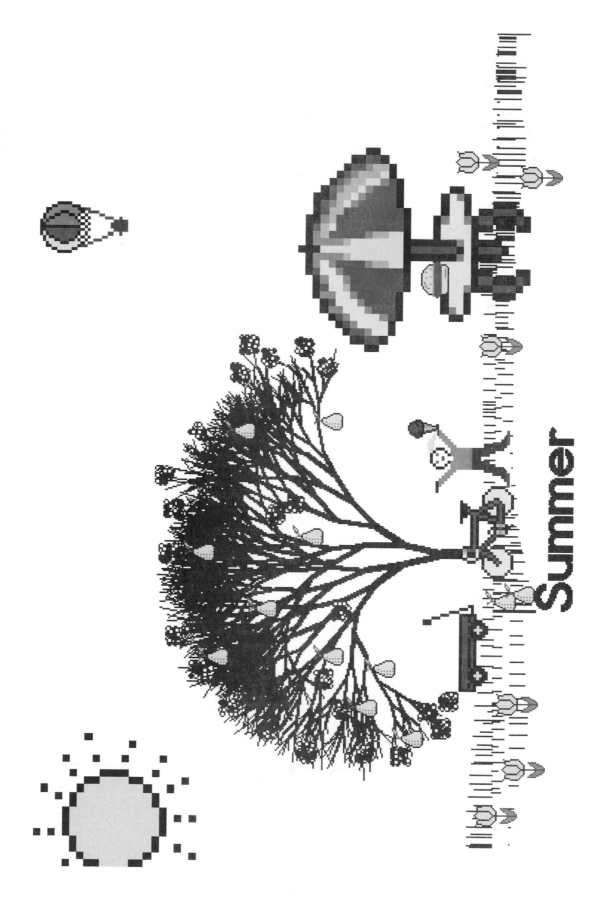

Summer

A Year in the Life of a Tree *(cont.)*

A Year in the Life of a Tree

We jump in her leaves in the fall. Even the Halloween ghost likes to swing in my tree.

In winter the snow covers her branches and is on the ground. We ski near her.

My tree is happy in the spring. The new leaves are coming. The grass is green all around her. My friends and I smell her blossoms.

In the summer we all play under her branches. Sometimes we eat near her. Her fruit tastes good to eat.

A Year in the Life of a Tree (cont.)

The Fraction Machine

During this activity students will be investigating the relationships between fractions. They will learn that a fraction represents a part of a "whole" and can be represented as a number.

Grade Level: three to five

Duration: 60–120 minutes on the computer

Materials: computer, clip art, Fraction Screen Chart (pages 248 and 250)

Software: *AppleWorks (ClarisWorks)*, *MSWorks*, *Kid Pix*, *Astound®* or other drawing type of program

Internet Links: *http://forum.swarthmore.edu/paths/fractions/e.fracdrmathstud.html*

Procedure: For Activity #1

Before the Computer

- Students should have a fair understanding of what a "whole" means. Have them understand clearly that nearly anything can be called one whole, even groups of items like 5 dogs, 3 candy bars or 1 pie.

- In the first part of this activity, students will be making fractions using clip art and their own drawings. Students will create fractions by taking a group of objects and calling them one whole. Then they will separate some of these objects from the whole and say what part of the whole they represent. Teachers should go over the concept of fractions with students before they start their drawings. Students should be clear on the terms numerator and denominator. Fractions are easier to draw if they are grouped by multiples.

On the Computer

- Students should look at these samples which were done in *Kid Pix*. In the first example, there are a total of 4 apples. Two of these apples have a line drawn around them. This means that the two represents the part and the four represents the whole. This is called two-fourths and it is written as 2/4.

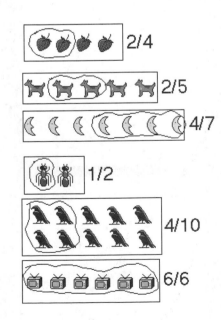

- While students are on the computer during this session, they will be creating fractions just like these. Students should label each fraction just as these have been labeled. If they are confused about what to do, they should talk to one of the classroom experts or ask for the teacher's assistance.

- Students should print their screen results and turn them in with their Fraction Screen Chart on page 248.

The Fraction Machine *(cont.)*

Fraction Screen Chart-Activity #1

- Create the following fractions on your computer with any drawing program.

2/3	two-thirds	5/10	five-tenths
1/6	one-sixth	8/8	eight-eighths
4/8	four-eighths	6/7	six-sevenths
3/9	three-ninths	4/5	four-fifths
2/7	two-sevenths	1/3	one-third

- Draw each screen using the form below. You should label each screen with the fraction it represents. Turn this chart in with your computer printout of the created fractions.

Show your fraction screens here. Label each fraction.

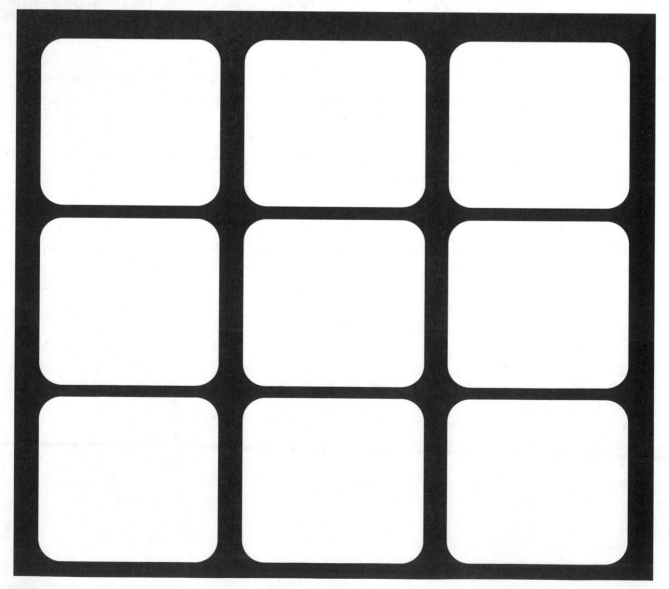

Fractions in a Box

Procedure: For Activity #2

Before the Computer

- For the first activity, students created fractions by taking a group of objects and calling them one whole. Then they separated some of these objects from the whole and said what part of the whole they represented. In this activity, they are going to take one object and divide that object into **equal** pieces.

- If students have ever cut a whole cake or a whole pie into smaller equal pieces, they already know how to make fractions.

On the Computer

- In the drawing program, students should create a square shape that has a black outline and is hollow in the middle. Divide this shape into halves, fourths, eighths, or the amount necessary. Remember to make each division **equal**. When working with fractions, the parts of the whole must be equal. Students should print and turn in work once they have completed this section. If the program that students are using has an Auto Grid function, it should be turned on. This will make it much easier to create and divide the shapes.

Sample

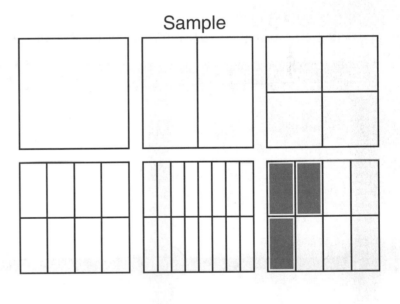

- In order to represent fractions, students should shade the part that they wish to be the numerator. In the sample, three out of a total of eight pieces have been shaded. This is called three-eighths or 3/8.

- Students should be clear about how to create fractions in this manner.

- Students should create the fractions found on the Fraction Screen Chart on page 250 in the manner just described here. They should not forget to label each fraction, to make each part equal, and to print the screen results when completed.

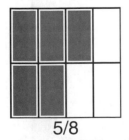
5/8

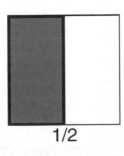
1/2

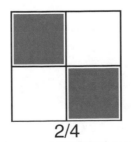
2/4

1

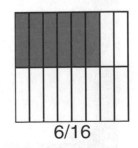
6/16

Fractions in a Box *(cont.)*

Fraction Screen Chart—Activity #2

- Create the following fractions on your computer with any drawing program.

2/3	two-thirds	5/6	five-sixths
4/7	four-sevenths	5/16	five-sixteenths
5/10	five-tenths	4/12	four-twelfths
1/9	one-ninth	3/9	three-ninths
2/5	two-fifths	1/4	one-fourth

- Draw each screen using the form below. You should label each screen with the fraction it represents. Turn this chart in with the printout from your computer.

Show your fraction screens here. Label each fraction.

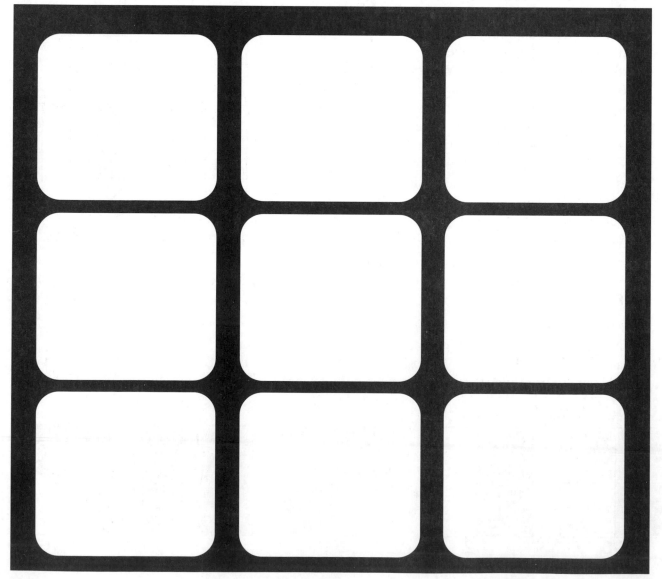

Mystery Squares

Students will be creating their own mystery squares using a drawing program.

Grade Level:	three to five
Duration:	30–60 minutes
Materials:	computer, Mystery Cube Planning Sheet (page 252)
Software:	Drawing program such as *Kid Pix*, *AppleWorks (ClarisWorks)*, etc.
Internet Link:	*http://www.oise.utoronto.ca/~wteo/humour.htm*

Procedure: For Activity #1

Before the Computer

- Students will need to be familiar with a drawing program and the tools available. If they have not worked with these programs before, teachers should go through a sample lesson with them.

- Depending on the age level, students may use addition or other math functions in their mystery cubes. After they create the cubes, they should print them out.

- Go over the example to the right with students. Notice that the sum of each pair of numbers is always 10. Notice that the sum of the three numbers moving horizontally always equals 15. This may look easy to do, but combinations take some thought. Students should use the Mystery Cube Planning Sheet on page 252 before going to the computers.

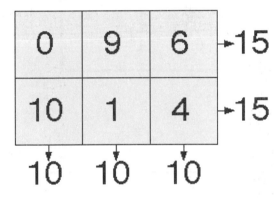

On the Computer

- As they create the mystery cubes, they will need to make sure that they can solve them. The printed version **should not** include the answers, just the requirements, such as "must add up to 10."

- The mystery squares can become more complicated when more squares are added. You may also require that both directions equal the same number as well as the diagonals. This is even more difficult.

A More Complex Example

- Two new elements have now been added to the mystery square. First, there is a 3 x 3 layout with nine locations for numbers. Second, all rows and columns must add up to 15. Finally, only the numbers 1–9 are allowed and no number can be repeated. When they design their magic cube, they should leave the numbers out and print the empty cube with the desired totals.

Mystery Squares *(cont.)*

Mystery Cube Planning Sheet

Use the planning templates below to help you design some mystery squares. Notice that different shapes have been generated. The rules and results are left entirely up to you and your teacher. After completing the planning sheet, go to the computer and create your Mystery Cubes.

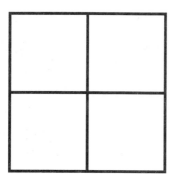
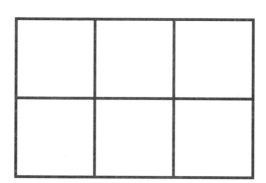

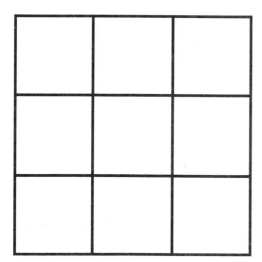
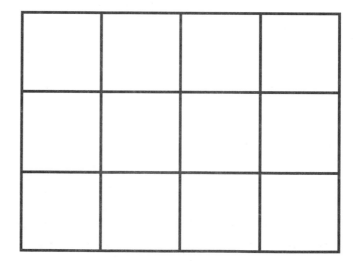

It All Adds Up

Using the computer, students will combine coins to come up with as many possible ways to make $1.00 as they can find.

Grade Level: three to five

Duration: 40–60 minutes on the computer

Materials: samples of U.S. coins, Color Code and Combinations Chart (page 254)

Software: any drawing program such as *Kid Pix, Hyperstudio®, Appleworks (ClarisWorks)* (must be able to move objects)

Internet Links: *http://pages.prodigy.com/kidsmoney/kids.htm*
http://www.usmint.gov/

Before the Computer

- Start this activity by providing students, either in groups or individually, with samples of all current U.S. coins. Attempt to get all students to differentiate between a half dollar, quarter, dime, nickel, and penny. Also discuss the relative values that these coins have (one nickel equals five pennies, one dime equals two nickels, etc.).

On the Computer

- Each student will create 2 half dollars, 4 quarters, 10 dimes, 10 nickels, and 10 pennies. Students must keep the proportions between the coins the same (i.e. a dime is not bigger than a nickel). Using the Copy and Paste functions found in nearly all drawing programs will make this an easy task.

- Students may want to make each coin a different color and create a color code to differentiate between coins.

- Once all of the coins have been created, the task is to combine them in as many ways as possible so that the **sum** equals $1.00. The student must move the coins around on the screen to come up with a combination that totals $1.00. Record this combination on the sheet that is found on the next page, and then look for other combinations. After all possible combinations have been found, be sure to **save their work**.

Challenge

- What combination requires the greatest number of coins to make a sum equal to $1.00? With a partner, students can move several different coins to the center of the screen and try to tell what the value is of these coins. Find out what all of the coins add up to!

Assessment

- Students should print out the computer screen and answer these questions in complete sentences, either at the bottom of the paper or on the back. Turn in this chart.

  1. What was the most difficult part of this activity?
  2. Is there another way to do this activity?
  3. Make up a game to play with a partner, using what was created on the computer screen.

It All Adds Up *(cont.)*

Color Code Chart: Use this chart to make a color code of the coins.

COIN	Half Dollar	Quarter	Dime	Nickel	Penny
COLOR					

Fill in this chart with combinations that equal $1.00.

Attempts	Half Dollar	Quarter	Dime	Nickel	Penny	Total $
#1	2					$1.00

Not Your Average Board Game

During this activity, students will be creating a board game that can be used to learn the process of finding averages. Students will work with rating scales.

Grade Level:	three to five
Duration:	90–120 minutes on the computer
Materials:	computer, clip art, game pieces, Not Your Average Board Game Score Sheet (page 257)
Software:	*AppleWorks (ClarisWorks)*, *MSWorks*, *Kid Pix* or other drawing software
Internet Links:	*http://www.blueberry.co.uk/thehill/nonshocked/games/index.html*
	http://www.astro.virginia.edu/~eww6n/math/math.html (go to Search and type Mean)

Before the Computer

- In the event that some students have never seen a board game before, teachers might want to show them a few samples of popular games.

- During this activity, students will be creating a board game by following very specific directions. Part of the assessment will take into consideration how well they followed those directions. Teachers can easily illustrate the importance of step-by-step directions by bringing in directions for assembling many different kinds of items that are sold unassembled today.

On the Computer

- Follow each of these steps in order. Try to do them exactly as they are written.

- On a blank drawing screen, create a square shape that is 5" x 5" (13 cm x 13 cm). If the program has an "Auto Grid" function, one that automatically sets the lines at defined intervals, students should use it.

- From each corner draw a straight line 1 inch (2.54 cm) in from the outside edge of the square.

- The shape should now look like figure A.

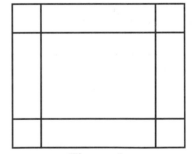

Figure A

- At 1 inch (2.54 cm) intervals, students are now going to fill in the shape along the outside edge. The four corners will later become special places.

- Their drawings should now look something like the one pictured in Figure B.

- They can add color to the corners by using a Fill tool. Students will also notice that some graphics have been added in the center of the game board as well as a title.

Figure B

Not Your Average Board Game *(cont.)*

On the Computer *(cont.)*

- Now students are ready to add their special places at the corners. Make one corner the Start location. This can be done by placing a large S at this location. Here is what the other three corners will say:

    1. Roll Again—roll the dice again.

    2. Skip a Turn—skip your turn this time; you cannot score a point.

    3. Earn a Free Point—earn a free point.

- Later, students can change these corner titles to something else if they wish. The game board should now look something like the first example on this page.

- The last thing that needs to be done is to fill in the numbers that will be used on the game board. If students want to make this board reusable, they should laminate it first so that students who use it later can change the numbers if they wish. They will need to use a marker or pen that is erasable.

- Students in third grade may want to stick with only one and two digit numbers, such as 7, 24, 54, and 9. Make sure that every blank space has a number. Students in grades 4 and 5 should use numbers with 2, 3, and 4 digits, such as 24, 487, 3,278, and 44.

- The board should now look like the second example, and students will be ready to play once they have printed it out and read the rules on page 257.

- Students will need one die. In order to check and score answers, students may want to have either a computer calculator or a desktop one available.

Follow-up Activities

- Without making any modification, this same activity could be used for addition, number sequence (from greatest to least, from least to greatest), fractions (regular or irregular), and ratio/proportion. The numbers will need to be changed to fit the skill on which students wish to work.

- Now that students have some experience in creating a computer math game, see if they can come up with other designs. Then have them write clear directions for the use of their creations.

- Self-assessment, which was used in this activity, is a good way to find out what students think and how they feel about their work. This kind of strategy can be used in some of the other activities found in this book.

Not Your Average Board Game *(cont.)*

Game Rules

- Decide who will go first. Using a die, the first player takes a turn and records the number. The first player goes again and records the second number. The first player goes a third time and records the third number. To find the average, the three numbers are added together and then divided by three. The other players perform a check to see if the answer is correct. When using a calculator, students should remember the rules regarding the rounding of numbers. If the answer is correct, this is marked on the score sheet. The player doing the averaging cannot use a calculator.

- It is now the second player's turn. Repeat the steps described above. If there are more than two players, each of them will repeat the steps described above.

- If students land on Skip a Turn on any of their three chances to move, they cannot score and must give up their turn to the next person. If they land on Earn a Free Point, they should give themselves a point on their score sheet. If they land on Roll Again, first they must finish the turn they are on and then go again. If they happen to land on Roll Again while in their second turn, they get to go another time.

Not Your Average Board Game Score Sheet

Player Name	Scoring Section (Check off one box for each correct answer.)
_____ _____	☐ ☐
_____ _____	☐ ☐ ☐ ☐ ☐ ☐ ☐ ☐ ☐ ☐ ☐ ☐ ☐ ☐ ☐ ☐ ☐ ☐ ☐ ☐
_____ _____	☐ ☐
_____ _____	☐ ☐ ☐ ☐ ☐ ☐ ☐ ☐ ☐ ☐ ☐ ☐ ☐ ☐ ☐ ☐ ☐ ☐ ☐ ☐

The Olympics

Objective

Let the games begin! Students apply their math skills to calculate the number of years ago the first Olympics began, as well as the number of years they lasted. They begin to consider differences between the ancient and modern games in the classroom and then go online to learn more differences, as well as reading about actual ancient Olympians.

Materials

- calculators (optional)
- one copy of page 262 for each student

Focus Web Site—Destination URLs

The Ancient Olympics
http://olympics.tufts.edu/

About This Site: Go back in time (way back in time) to the first Olympic events. Select from seven related links to investigate the manner in which the ancient games compare to the modern Olympic games, including a guided tour of the original site of the Olympics.

Alternative Web Sites

The Ancient Olympic Games Virtual Museum
http://devlab.dartmouth.edu/olympic/

First Olympic Games—Athens 1896
http://orama.com/athens1896/

Olympic Golden Nuggets
http://www.cam.org/~fishon1/olympic.html

Author's Note: The men who competed in the ancient games did so without clothing. Some of the graphics (mostly etchings, carvings, and cartoons) reveal the Olympians from a front or side view. Use discretion when accessing these sites with students.

The Olympics *(cont.)*

Pre-Internet Activity

Lead a discussion about the students' favorite Olympic sports and competitors. Ask them to identify the location of the most recent Olympic games. Explain that the Olympics began in Greece in 776 B.C. Ask the students to recall the prizes the winners received. Explain that early victors were awarded head wreaths made of olive tree branches. Ask students to recall some sports of the modern Olympic games. Explain that the very first Olympics had only one running event but soon included numerous running events and other sports. Tell the students that they will have a chance to further investigate the differences between the ancient and modern Olympic games on the Internet, as well as read about an actual ancient Olympian.

Teaching the Lesson

1. Help students discover how many years ago the first Olympics took place. Have them consider all the advancements and changes the world has witnessed throughout that time. Besides the above-mentioned comparisons, how else do the students think the ancient Olympics differed from the modern games?

2. Explain that the ancient Olympics ended around 394 A.D. Help the students calculate the duration of the ancient Olympics. (*1,170 years*) Explain that in this amount of time, many changes took place in the games. They will compare this period of time known as the "ancient" Olympics to the "modern" games which date back to 1896, only a little over one hundred years ago.

3. Distribute a copy of page 263 to each student. If desired, access the Web site as a class and link to **Ancient and Modern Olympic Sports**. Read the information there and have students complete numbers 1, 2, and 3 on their sheets.

4. Divide the class into five groups and assign each team to access one of the five ancient Olympians listed at the **Stories** link, or have the students work with a partner to access this link and select an Olympian of their choice. Have the students share their research with the class.

Olympic Background Information

- The Greek calendar was based on the Olympiad (four-year interval between games).

- Hercules founded the games.

- Temples and statues were erected to honor Zeus.

- The games were canceled during WWI (1916) and WWII (1940 and 1944).

- In 1992, the winter and summer games began alternating every two years.

The Ancient Olympic Games

Launch this Web site: *http://olympics.tufts.edu/*

Directions: The original Olympics were very different from the events the world celebrates in modern times. Read about how they were different by selecting the link "Ancient and Modern Olympic Sports." List three ways the ancient Olympics were different from the modern games.

Ancient Games   **Modern Games**

1. _____   _____

   _____   _____

2. _____   _____

   _____   _____

3. _____   _____

   _____   _____

Click the **Stories** link. Select a name of an ancient Olympian. Read his story and then complete the information below.

His name: _____

His sport: _____

Year(s) he participated: _____

How he became an Olympian: _____

_____

_____

_____

_____

_____

_____

_____

_____

_____

Egyptian Facts from the Internet

Objectives

- Learning the meaning of global addresses
- Typing a specific global address and finding the site
- Copying and pasting Internet pictures into another program
- Working with more than one program at the same time

Program Needed

You will need access to the Internet and a program which you can draw boxes and type in the boxes such as *AppleWorks (ClarisWorks)* (under Drawing) or *Microsoft Publisher*.

Instructions

1. Students will launch the Internet. If time permits, show students other Internet addresses such as **http://www.disney.com** or **http://www.weather.com/twc/homepage.twc**

2. Type the address **http://www.clemusart.com/archive/pharoah/rosetta.index.html** which will send them to the Rosetta Stone Exhibit at the Cleveland Art Museum.

3. Students will scroll down and click on **FACT/FICTION**.

4. Then students will open a blank *AppleWorks (ClarisWorks)* (Drawing file) or *Publisher* page.

5. Students will draw boxes and label the boxes in a way that is similar to those on the next page (pyramids, hieroglyphs, mummies, etc.).

6. Students will go back into the Internet and find facts about pyramids.

7. Students will open their pages with the boxes and rewrite this fact about pyramids in their own words. Students will continue going back and forth between programs until all boxes are completed.

8. Have students copy pictures from the Internet page to fill in blank areas. To copy and paste an Internet picture on a Macintosh, simply click on the picture and hold down the mouse. A pull-down menu will appear; click on "Copy This Image." Then launch *AppleWorks (ClarisWorks)* or *Microsoft Word* and click on Edit, Paste. To do this on a PC is a bit more involved. Consult the manual.

9. Spell check and print the completed page with the boxes on it.

Extension Ideas

Students can make fact sheets like this Egypt one with any subject matter. This is also a great way for students to share how they celebrate the holidays.

Facts About Egypt

Pyramids

Pyramids were graves for the Egyptian kings. The Egyptians thought the pyramids honored the king and protected him from any harm.

Mummies

A mummy is a dead body which is preserved in a special way so the body doesn't rot. The tradition of mummification was overseen by the priests in Egypt.

Hieroglyphs

An important breakthrough for the understanding of hieroglyphics was the discovery of the Rosetta Stone in 1799. The stone is a piece of black granite with the same writing written in three different scripts, one script being hieroglyphic.

Other Facts

1. The stem of the papyrus plants was used to make Egyptian paper.

2. The Egyptians primarily ate bread. Skeletons show their teeth were worn down by the bread they ate.

3. Egyptians were quite concerned about their appearance. They wore makeup, perfume, and fine garments.

Welcome to My Travel Agency

Because you love to travel, you have started your own travel agency. In order for your travel agency to be successful, you will need to entice travelers to want to travel to the destinations you can provide. Brainstorm a list of destinations. After you choose one, research as much as you can about the location using reference books and/or the computer. Once you have decided on your destination and have collected interesting information, it's time for you to create a travel brochure. Your brochure will need to be colorful and attractive and include lots of interesting facts. Your brochure will be a trifold (paper folded into thirds). You may do all the work by hand. Or, if available, you may do the work on a computer. The pages that follow tell you how to create a hand drawn or computer generated brochure.

Hand Drawn Brochure

1. Research and gather the following information about your particular destination: location and history, unique items produced in the area, places of interest, a map of the area, special foods, transportation, dress, recreation, etc.

2. You may create the panels for your brochure on separate paper and glue them onto your brochure. Suggestion: Use an 8 ½" x 11" (22 cm x 28 cm) piece of color construction paper folded into thirds as your brochure.

3. Create a cover for the first panel showing some of the sites to see.

4. On one of the travel brochure panels, you may want to include a map and some history of the place.

5. On several panels, describe tourist sites of interest, places to shop and eat, and places to stay at while visiting.

6. Draw a citizen in traditional dress on another panel or some of the recreational activities that people can do when they visit the destination.

7. Be sure to include the name of the travel agency and how travelers can contact you on the last panel.

8. Decorate your brochure with pencils, markers, color pencils, crayons, stickers, glitter, etc.

Welcome to My Travel Agency *(cont.)*

Computer Generated Brouchure

When people are deciding where to take a vacation, they may consult with a travel agent and/or read brochures about potential vacation places. These brochures are created to attract those tourists. Tourism is a great source of income to many countries.

You are going to create a travel brochure that would entice someone to plan a vacation in your chosen area. You will need to find out some information about the place that you choose. This is a creative activity designed to create a travel brochure on *Kid Pix*.

1. Research the area that you have chosen:

    - **location and history**

    - **things to buy that are unique**

    - **places of interest**

    - **map of the area**

    - **special foods**

    - **transportation**

    - **manner of dress**

    - **types of recreation**

2. This brochure is going to be a trifold. A trifold has six sides. You will divide the first screen into three sections and design each individual section. After printing the first page, you will then do the same thing on the second page. After both pages are printed, cut them apart and glue them onto a piece of construction paper to complete your brochure.

Front Side   **Back Side**

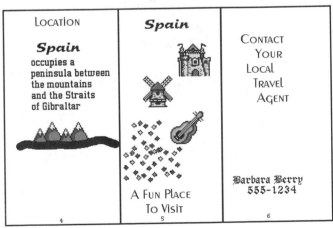

Welcome to My Travel Agency *(cont.)*

3. Divide the screen into thirds. Select the Line tool, hold down the shift key and divide the screen.

4. The section on the far left will be your cover. Use the Type Text tool from the GOODIES menu in *Kid Pix*. If you are using *Kid Pix Studio*, select the Typewriter tool. Type in an inviting phrase to make people want to read the rest of your brochure.

5. Add a graphic by using the Rubber Stamp tool and options that will help illustrate your place.

6. The middle section is for showing things that you can do in the place that you are telling people about. Title this section, "Things to Do."

7. Using the Rubber Stamp tool, select some options that will help show the things that a tourist can do at this place.

8. The final panel is to show the places that tourists can visit while on vacation. Title this section, "Places to Go." Now add graphics to show some of these places to go.

9. Save your work and print your page.

10. Fold a piece of construction paper into thirds.

11. Cut your page along the solid line. You now have three panels for your brochure. Glue the Cover, Things to Do page, and the Places to Go page onto the construction paper. You now have one half of the brochure completed.

12. Clear your screen and follow the directions in #1.

13. Label the first section "Location and History." Include information about the location and history of your vacation place.

14. On the middle section, explain why your vacation place is a fun place to visit.

15. On the last section, tell your potential customers where and how they can arrange for their trip.

16. Print your page. Cut apart your three sections and place them on a piece of construction paper which has been folded in thirds.

Welcome to My Travel Agency *(cont.)*

Places to Go

3

Things to Do

OLE!

2

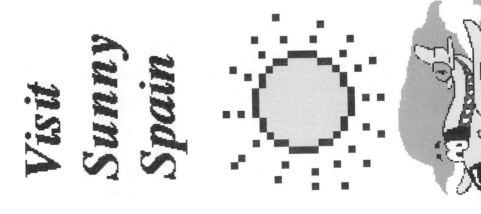

Visit Sunny Spain

1

Welcome to My Travel Agency *(cont.)*

Location

Spain

occupies a peninsula between the mountains and the Straits of Gibraltar

4

Spain

A Fun Place To Visit

5

Contact Your Local Travel Agent

𝔅𝔞𝔯𝔟𝔞𝔯𝔞 𝔅𝔢𝔯𝔯𝔶
555–1234

6

Center Signs

Language Arts

Center Signs *(cont.)*

Math

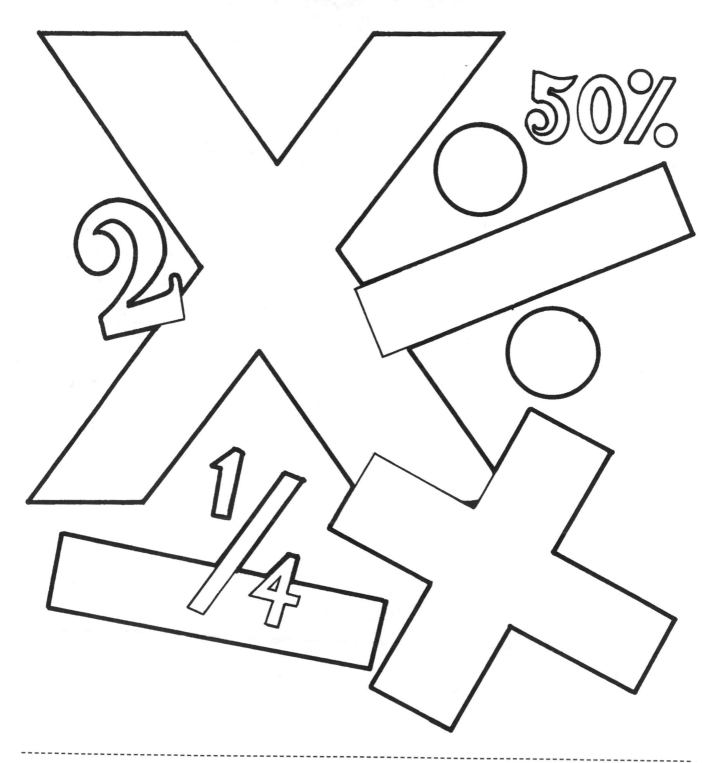

Center Signs (cont.)

Science

Center Signs (cont.)

Social Studies

Center Signs *(cont.)*

Games & Puzzles

Center Signs *(cont.)*

Technology

Center Signs *(cont.)*

This center is open.

Center Signs *(cont.)*

This center is closed.

Center Signs *(cont.)*

Writing

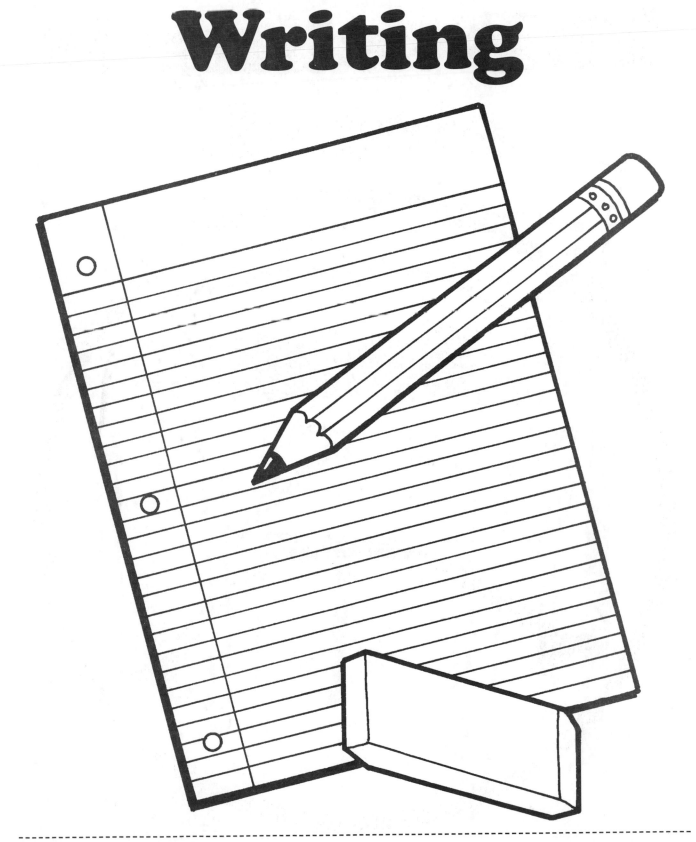

Center Signs *(cont.)*

Reading

Center Signs *(cont.)*

Center Signs *(cont.)*

Center Signs *(cont.)*

Computer
Sign
Up

Center Signs *(cont.)*

Center Supplies

Answer Key

Page 27

This is a very sad story because it is about two people who love each other very much and want to marry, but they have never been able to do so.

Sun loves Moon more than life itself. He knows she is the most beautiful being ever seen on earth. Sun would give everything he has if only he could win her for his wife.

Alas, the one time he asked her to marry him, she said, "Oh, yes! I will marry you, but there is one thing you must do first."

"Anything!" Sun answered. "I will do anything you say, for I love you very much. Just tell me what it is."

Moon told him, "To prove your love for me, you must bring me a gift that fits me exactly."

"What gift would you like me to bring?"

"It can be anything to wear, but it must fit me exactly," Moon replied.

Time and time again Sun comes with a gift for Moon to wear, but one time the gift is too small, and the next time it is too large. It is never exactly the right size. This happens each time Sun comes with a gift for Moon to wear. So on and on Sun tries with gift after gift. When you see Sun crying, you must know it is because he loves Moon more than anything, but he can never marry her.

Page 28

One day Turkey was walking on a trail through the woods when, by chance, he met Terrapin. Turkey, who wears a red flowing wattle and carries his head high in the air, thinks he is better than other people.

When he saw Terrapin with his slow, clumsy gait and the hard-shelled house he carries on his back, he could not resist the opportunity to bring him down a peg or two.

"What on earth are you good for?" Turkey asked in his usual snobbish way.

"I am good for many things," Terrapin replied. "I can beat you in a race!"

"Ha, ha, ha!" laughed Turkey. "That is the silliest thing I have ever heard! You beat me in a race! Ha, ha, ha!"

So they had a race. They met at the edge of the village. Because all terrapins look alike in their shell houses, Terrapin was to carry a white feather in his mouth so he would be different from all the other terrapins. They began.

Turkey did not know Terrapin had a lot of friends and they all think alike and get along with each other. At each hill, a friend was waiting with a white feather in his mouth to carry on a relay to the end of the race.

Meanwhile, Turkey walked slowly along, sure he would win. Much to his surprise, as he neared the finish line, he saw Terrapin crossing it. He never figured out why.

Can you?

Page 43

Answers will vary.

Page 44

Answers will vary.

Page 50

bacteria—one-celled germ

bamboozle—trick or cheat

barrack—building for lodging soldiers

catastrophe—major disaster

decline—refuse

edible—able to be eaten

entice—to attract or tempt

gondola—water taxi

Answer Key (cont.)

headquarters—center of operations

molt—to shed skin

outcast—one rejected by society

prohibit—forbid

Page 52

Answers will vary.

Page 54 and 55

Do you want some ice cream?

Yes, I want to go.

The house is on fire!

We went to Paris, France.

My dog's name is Chubba.

What is your favorite movie?

"I'm hungry!" said Fred.

School starts at 8:15.

She was cold; she put on a jacket.

It is Joe's cat.

Help!

Sue said, "I like chocolate cake."

They went to sleep at 10:30.

Maria had to have an x-ray taken.

Page 58 and Page 59

Answers will vary.

Page 61

Answers will vary.

Page 66

Woodrow Wilson

Pages 67 and 68

Answers will vary.

Page 69

1. $9.65
2. $3.53
3. $2.55
4. $2.65
5. $13.00
6. $27.00

Page 71

For metric answers, convert the following U.S. customary responses accordingly.

A1. 7,000,000,000

A2. the population of the United States.

A3. an almanac

A4. Divide the number of cookies by the population figures.

B1. 90 million over 150 million; three-fifths

B2. 50 million; find out what fraction 30 million is of 90 million - one-third - and find one-third of 150 million to get 50 million

C1. Divide 150 million pounds by 10 to get 15 million pounds.

C2. One solution: You already know that 150 million cookies equals 10 times around the globe. Fifteen times is half again as much as ten, so divide 150 million by 2. Add that figure to 150 million. The equation will read 150 million + 75 million = 225 million.

D1. Multiply 33,000 by 7, which is the number of days in a week, to get 231,000.

D2. Divide 33,000 by 24 to get 1,375.

Page 72–74

Answers will vary.

Answer Key (cont.)

Page 77 and 78

1. 8 ft.
2. 34 cm
3. 961 cm^2
4. 9 m
5. 12 in.
6. 102 ft.
7. 7 m
8. 162 ft.^{2}

Page 86

1. $6 + 4 - 1 - 2 + 6 + 2 = 15$ (or)
   $6 + 4 - 1 + 2 + 6 - 2 = 15$
2. $9 + 1 - 3 + 1 - 4 + 1 = 5$ (or)
   $9 - 1 + 3 - 1 - 4 - 1 = 5$
3. $9 - 3 + 4 - 1 + 2 + 3 = 14$
4. $5 - 1 + 1 + 3 + 4 - 6 = 6$
5. $9 - 8 + 6 + 3 - 5 + 3 = 8$
6. $2 - 1 + 8 + 9 - 3 + 5 = 20$
7. $5 + 3 + 2 - 4 + 1 + 5 = 12$
8. $4 + 9 + 3 - 7 + 3 - 1 = 11$
9. $7 - 6 + 2 + 8 - 7 - 1 = 3$
10. $9 + 9 - 9 + 2 - 2 - 8 = 1$ (or)
    $9 - 9 + 9 - 2 + 2 - 8 = 1$

Page 87

1. $9 - 8 + 6 + 3 - 5 + 1 = 6$
2. $5 - 3 + 4 + 4 - 2 + 9 = 17$
3. $5 + 3 + 2 - 4 + 1 - 5 = 2$ (or)
   $5 - 3 + 2 + 4 - 1 - 5 = 2$
4. $3 + 2 - 1 + 4 + 1 - 3 = 6$
5. $5 - 1 - 1 + 3 + 4 + 8 = 18$
6. $4 + 9 - 3 + 7 + 3 - 1 = 19$
7. $2 - 1 + 8 + 9 - 3 + 5 = 20$
8. $8 + 7 + 1 - 4 - 4 + 6 = 14$ (or)
   $8 - 7 - 1 + 4 + 4 + 6 = 14$

9. $7 - 6 + 2 + 9 - 9 - 3 = 0$
10. $3 + 5 - 3 + 9 + 6 - 5 = 15$

Page 88

1. $75 \div 3 \times 4 \div 2 \times 100 \div 250 = 20$
2. $15 \times 6 \div 9 \times 3 \times 4 \div 10 = 12$
3. $6 \times 8 \div 12 \times 3 \times 6 \div 9 = 8$
4. $144 \div 12 \times 3 \div 6 \times 5 \div 10 = 3$
5. $14 \times 64 \div 8 \div 8 \times 4 \div 4 = 14$
6. $32 \div 8 \div 1 \times 10 \times 3 \div 10 = 12$
7. $44 \div 11 \times 7 \times 2 \div 7 \times 11 = 88$
8. $81 \div 3 \div 9 \times 3 \times 7 \div 21 = 3$
9. $18 \div 9 \times 4 \times 7 \div 4 \div 2 = 7$
10. $100 \div 10 \times 3 \div 5 \div 3 \times 15 = 30$

Page 89

1. $81 \div 9 \times 7 \div 21 \times 6 \div 2 = 9$
2. $12 \div 6 \times 2 \div 12 \div 4 \times 5 = 15$
3. $88 \div 11 \times 3 \div 4 \times 12 \div 8 = 9$
4. $108 \div 4 \div 9 \times 5 \times 6 \div 30 = 3$
5. $54 \div 9 \times 6 \times 2 \div 8 \times 15 = 135$
6. $32 \times 2 \div 8 \times 12 \div 3 \div 2 = 16$
7. $15 \div 5 \times 7 \times 3 \div 7 \times 5 = 45$
8. $91 \div 13 \div 3 \times 5 \times 4 \div 21 = 20$
9. $13 \times 11 \times 5 \times 2 \div 6 \times 21 = 105$
10. $100 \div 100 \times 12 \times 2 \times 3 \div 9 = 8$

Page 90

1. 771; ill
2. 7735; sell
3. 35001; loose
4. 710; oil
5. 0.7734; hello
6. 0.02; zoo
7. 376616; giggle

Answer Key (cont.)

8. 3045; shoe

9. 808; Bob

10. 0.40404; hohoho

11. 3704; hole

12. 7105; soil

13. 638; beg

14. 505; SOS

15. 0.6; go

Page 91

1. 35,001; loose

2. 38,076; globe

3. 5,338; bees

4. 710; oil

5. 3,504; hose

6. 771; ill

7. 0.04008; boohoo

8. 7,718; Bill

9. 35,108; Boise

10. 618; big

Page 92

Students may find a variety of paths, but the only boxes included in the maze should be the following:

First column: boxes 2 and 3

Second column: boxes 4, 5, and 7

Third column: boxes 3, 4, 6, and 7

Fourth column: boxes 2, 5, and 7

Page 93

1. motion

2. kinetic

3. Wind

4. energy

5. Hcat

6. Sound

7. Electricity

8. changed

Page 94

1. 120

2. 10

3. triangle

4. tells time

5. 4,000

6. colon

7. 12

8. 6

9. sum

10. 100

11. 6

12. octagon

13. 6

14. 10

15. 24

Page 95

1. graph

2. 90 degrees

3. time zone

4. 100

5. octagon

6. 10

7. 40

8. 21

9. no

Answer Key *(cont.)*

10. 10

11. 6

12. length x width

13. 606

14. 70

15. 360 degrees

Page 96

1. no
2. 300
3. It means having the same size and shape.
4. They weigh the same.
5. CLXXVI
6. protractor
7. 5
8. 144
9. 10
10. 3/4
11. 9
12. obtuse
13. yes
14. a straight line
15. ordinal

Page 97

1. 1,000
2. M
3. tangram
4. 5,280
5. minimum
6. 12.5 or 12 1/2
7. 1/2
8. 24
9. radius

10. 7

11. 9

12. multiply the number by itself

13. 7 tenths

14. acute

15. prime number

Page 98

Answers will vary.

Page 100

1. prophet
2. vaccine
3. soldier
4. Braille
5. Dodgers
6. New Deal
7. aviator
8. Hershey
9. skating
10. peanuts
11. authors
12. villain
13. dancing
14. senator
15. chemist

Page 101

1. add
2. sum
3. zero
4. half
5. plus
6. minus
7. addition

Answer Key (cont.)

8. negative

9. digit

10. mathematics

11. subtract

12. times

13. divide

14. fraction

15. number

Page 102

1. False
2. True
3. False
4. False
5. False
6. False
7. False
8. True
9. False
10. True

Page 103

1. 12
2. 13
3. 5 rings
4. 100 years
5. 13 colonies
6. 5 sides
7. 1 wheel
8. 168 hours
9. 366 days
10. 1,000 years
11. 52 cards
12. 100 centimeters

13. 90 degrees

14. 9 planets

15. 1 eye

16. 88 keys

17. 206 bones

18. 360 degrees

19. 10 events

20. 64 squares

Page 116

1. platypus
2. dingo
3. emu
4. kangaroo
5. koala
6. wombat
7. wallaby
8. cuscus

Page 117

Animal	Male	Female	Young	Group
fox	dog	vixen	cub	skulk
chicken	rooster	hen	chick	flock
lion	lion	lioness	cub	pride
cattle	bull	cow	calf	herd
whale	bull	cow	calf	pod
seal	bull	cow	pup	herd
ostrich	cock	hen	chick	flock
sheep	ram	ewe	lamb	herd
goose	gander	goose	gosling	gaggle
kangaroo	buck	doe	joey	herd
hog	boar	sow	piglet	herd
goat	billy	nanny	kid	herd

Answer Key (cont.)

Page 119

1. Nome: 0° to 10° F/-18° to -12° C

   Kodiak: Above 32° F/Above 0° C

   Barrow: Below -10° F/Below -23° C

   Anchorage: 0° to 10° F/-18° to -12° C

   Juneau: 10° to 32° F/-12° to 0° C

   Fairbanks: Below -10° F/Below -23° C

2. Barrow

   Fairbanks

   Nome

   Barrow

3. No

Page 123

1. the nervous system
2. Halley's comet
3. solid, liquid, and gas
4. a barometer
5. smog
6. the elbow
7. chlorophyll
8. kinetic energy
9. an earthquake
10. a carnivore
11. oxygen
12. hot
13. the esophagus
14. meteors
15. a crater

Page 124

1. thermometer
2. invertebrates
3. gills

4. oysters
5. telescope
6. Saturn
7. skunk
8. eight
9. hummingbirds
10. fog
11. tadpole
12. bats
13. school
14. toadstool
15. poles

Page 125

1. circulatory system
2. Venus
3. cold-blooded
4. solar and radiant
5. collarbone
6. 0° C
7. Mike Collins
8. tropical
9. Mercury
10. Sun
11. two
12. kangaroo
13. left ventricle
14. crater
15. herbivore

Page 126

1. True
2. True
3. True

Answer Key (cont.)

4. True

5. True

6. False

7. False

8. True

9. False

10. False

Page 127

1. True

2. True

3. True

4. False

5. True

6. False

7. True

8. False

9. False

10. True

Page 128

1. F

2. G

3. B

4. E

5. A

6. C

7. D

8. I

9. J

10. H

Page 129

1. astronaut

2. earth

3. clouds

4. hibernate

5. insect

6. moon

7. hurricane

8. rain

9. stomach

10. microscope

11. flowers

12. snow

13. thermometer

14. mammals

15. gravity

Page 131–133

Life Science	Earth Science
digestion	earthquake
skeleton	tornado
larynx	clay
cell	diamond
eardrum	climate
nervous system	gravity
blood	volcano
hibernation	

Answer Key (cont.)

Page 139

Major Group	Subgroup	Name	Picture
vertebrate	reptile	snake	
vertebrate	bird	duck	
vertebrate	fish	catfish	
vertebrate	amphibian	frog	
vertebrate	mammal	raccoon	
vertebrate	dinosauria	protoceratops	
invertebrate	worm	earthworm	
invertebrate	centipede/millipede	thousand leg	
invertebrate	insect	dragonfly	
invertebrate	crustacean	lobster	
invertebrate	snail	conch	
invertebrate	spider	brown spider	

Page 141

1. Elizabeth Blackwell
2. Julia Ward House
3. G. M. Pullman
4. Cyrus McCormick
5. Thomas Edison
6. Abner Doubleday
7. Walt Whitman
8. P. T. Barnum
9. Alexander G. Bell
10. A. S. Hallidie
11. E. G. Otis
12. George Westinghouse
13. F. W. Woolworth
14. Samuel Morse
15. Mark Twain

Page 142

1. Kodak camera
2. railroad sleeping car
3. printing from movable type
4. wireless telegraph
5. vulcanization of rubber
6. quick-freezing process of perserving food
7. dynamite
8. telephone
9. bifocal glasses
10. steel plow
11. first successful airplane
12. electric light
13. assembly line method of production
14. cotton gin
15. sewing machine

Page 143

1. My name is _____.
2. I am _____ years old.

Page 144

1. Columbus
2. Byrd
3. Cortez
4. Earhart
5. Darwin
6. Magellan
7. Cousteau
8. Balboa
9. Pizarro
10. Cartier
11. Armstrong
12. Hudson

Page 145

1. John
2. Dwight
3. Ronald

Answer Key *(cont.)*

4. Thomas

5. Richard

6. Abraham

7. Jimmy

8. Herbert

9. Theodore or Franklin

10. George

11. Calvin

12. Grover

13. Ulysses

14. Zachary

15. William or Benjamin

16. Harry

17. James

18. James

19. James

20. Lyndon or Andrew

Page 146

1. I

2. C

3. B

4. L

5. K

6. E

7. H

8. M

9. G

10. O

11. A

12. F

13. D

14. N

15. J

Page 147

1. Paul Revere

2. Abraham Lincoln

3. Robert E. Lee

4. Douglas MacArthur

5. Harriet Tubman

6. Johnny Appleseed

7. George Washington

8. Thomas Edison

9. Benjamin Franklin

10. Neil Armstrong

11. Amelia Earhart

12. Betsy Ross

Page 148

1. Guyana

2. Argentina

3. Venezuela

4. Bolivia

5. Uruguay

6. French Guiana

7. Suriname

8. Brazil

9. Peru

10. Chile

11. Paraguay

12. Colombia

13. Equador

Page 149 and 150

1. Florida

2. Alaska

3. Rhode Island

4. Minnesota, Wisconsin, Illinois, Missouri, Nebraska, South Dakota

Answer Key (cont.)

5. Kansas, Nebraska, South Dakota, North Dakota

6. Texas, Louisiana, Mississippi, Alabama, Florida

7. Hawaii

8. Idaho

9. Illinois

10. New York

11. Oregon, Nevada, Arizona

12. Minnesota, Mississippi, Missouri, Montana, Michigan, Maine, Maryland, Massachusetts

13. Maine, New Hampshire, Massachusetts, Connecticut, Rhode Island, New York, New Jersey, Delaware, Maryland, Virginia, North Carolina, South Carolina, Georgia, Florida

14. California, Oregon, Washington, Alaska, Hawaii

15. Minnesota, Wisconsin, Michigan, Illinois, Indiana, Ohio, Pennsylvania, New York

16. Alaska

17. Alaska

18. California, Arizona, New Mexico, Texas

19. Washington, Idaho, Montana, North Dakota, Minnesota, New York, Vermont, New Hampshire, Maine

20. Manhattan

Page 152 and 153

1. E
2. F
3. D
4. K
5. B
6. G
7. L
8. C
9. J
10. M
11. A
12. H
13. N
14. O
15. I
16. P

Page 156

1. Des Moines, Iowa—42° N, 94° W
2. London, England—51.5° N, 0
3. Guadalajara, Mexico—20.5° N, 103.5° W
4. Oslo, Norway—60° N, 11° E
5. Athens, Greece—38° N, 24° E
6. Capetown, South Africa
7. San Diego, CA
8. Paris, France
9. Toronto, Canada
10. Berlin, Germany
11. North America
12. Asia
13. South America
14. Australia
15. Europe
16. Africa
17. Africa
18. Europe
19. South America
20. Asia

Page 158

1. a singer and actor
2. yes; promoted higher education for African Americans
3. Atlanta, Georgia

Answer Key (cont.)

4. W. E. B. DuBois

5. bondage or forced servitude

6. New York

7. person who wants to abolish slavery

8. first African American Supreme Court justice

9. separation or isolation of an ethnic group or race

10. African Americans fought in the Civil War for the Union.

11. tennis

12. document which freed slaves in Confederate states during the Civil War

13. first African American baseball player in the Major Leagues

14. first African American in space

15. yes

Page 159

1. Lincoln and Washington

2. July 4

3. November

4. November 11

5. Labor Day

6. Memorial Day is to honor Americans who gave their lives for their country (Some people also use the day to honor all loved ones who have died.)

7. Columbus Day

8. Dr. Martin Luther King, Jr.

9. January 15 (or the third Monday of January)

10. St. Patrick's Day

11. Grandparent's Day

12. Citizenship Day

Page 160

1. North America

2. east

3. red

4. Mississippi River

5. north

6. Alexander Graham Bell

7. atlas

8. Mt. Everest

9. island

10. Nina, Pinta, and Santa Maria

11. Mt. Rushmore

12. Huron, Ontario, Michigan, Erie, and Superior

13. Peru

14. Pacific

15. Honolulu

Page 161

1. monarchy

2. United States and Britain

3. Sahara

4. South America

5. Denmark

6. Christopher Jones

7. Cuba

8. Hernando Cortez

9. Himalayas

10. Russia

11. topographic

12. Australia

13. 1914–1918

14. twelve

15. China

Page 162

1. France

Answer Key (cont.)

2. Germany

3. Mexico

4. France

5. Italy

6. Netherlands

7. Spain & California

8. Germany

9. Pennsylvania

10. England

11. South America

12. England

13. France

14. Border of Europe and Asia

15. England

Page 163

Accept place names that may be found in states other than those listed.

1. New York City, New York

2. Cambridge, Massachusetts

3. Lincoln, Nebraska

4. Plymouth, Massachusetts

5. Salisbury, Maryland

6. Reading, Massachusetts

7. New Bern, North Carolina

8. Birmingham, Alabama

9. Rome, Georgia

10. Paris, Texas

11. St. Petersburg, Florida

12. Manchester, New Hampshire

13. Athens, Georgia

14. Valencia, California

15. New Orleans, Louisiana

16. Waterloo, Iowa

17. Memphis, Tennessee

18. Odessa, Texas

19. Cleveland, Ohio

20. Frankfort, Kentucky

Page 164

1. Land of Lincoln, Springfield

2. Beehive State, Salt Lake City

3. Mountain State, Charleston

4. Lone Star State, Austin

5. Wolverine State, Lansing

6. First State, Dover

7. Bluegrass State, Frankfort

8. Last Frontier, Juneau

9. Green Mountain State, Montpelier

10. Ocean State and Little Rhody, Providence

11. Flickertail State, Bismarck

12. Empire State, Albany

13. Empire State of the South, Atlanta

14. Volunteer State, Nashville

15. Badger State, Madison

16. Sunflower State, Topeka

17. Hoosier State, Indianapolis

18. Constitution State, Hartford

19. Evergreen State, Olympia

20. Golden State, Sacramento

21. Land of Enchantment, Santa Fe

22. Gopher State, St. Paul

23. Keystone State, Harrisburg

24. Magnolia State, Jackson

25. Equality State, Cheyenne

Page 165

1. Alaska, California, Colorado, Illinois, Louisiana, Michigan, South Dakota, Texas, Utah

Answer Key (cont.)

2. Florida, Maine, Montana, North Carolina, Virginia

3. Florida, Georgia, Hawaii, Kentucky, North Carolina, Tennessee, Virginia

4. Florida (twice), Illinois, Kansas, Nebraska, North Carolina, Tennessee, Virginia

Page 167 and 168

1. South America
2. Europe
3. South America
4. South America
5. North America
6. South America
7. Asia
8. North America
9. Africa
10. Europe
11. Europe
12. Europe
13. Asia
14. Asia
15. Asia
16. Asia
17. Europe
18. Europe
19. Europe
20. Asia
21. Africa
22. Asia
23. Asia
24. Asia
25. Africa
26. Africa
27. Europe
28. Australia
29. South America
30. Africa
31. Europe
32. Asia
33. South America
34. Asia
35. Europe
36. Europe
37. Asia
38. Asia & Europe
39. Europe
40. Europe
41. Europe
42. Asia
43. North America
44. Asia & Europe
45. Europe

Page 179

1. Truman
2. Polk
3. Madison
4. Fillmore
5. Garfield
6. Taylor
7. Washington
8. Jackson
9. Coolidge
10. Hoover

Page 180

1. EZ
2. IC

Answer Key (cont.)

3. CU

4. P

5. C

6. K, D, or B

7. O

8. I

9. U or I

10. TP

11. IV

12. Y

13. T or OJ

14. B

15. DJ

Page 181

1. Q

2. XTC

3. NME

4. NV

5. B, D, K or L

6. O

7. SA

8. FX

9. J

10. CU

11. AT

12. T

13. G or O

14. XL

15. DK

Page 182

1. Hoover 3 Jefferson 1 Lincoln 2

2. 2/5 1 1/3 2 1/2 3

3. airplane 1 radio 2 television 3

4. Babe Ruth 1 Michael Jordan 3
Joe Namath 2

5. Civil War 2 Spanish American War 3
Revolutionary War 1

6. Elton John 3 Elvis 1 Beatles 2

7. Industrial Revolution 2 Westward Expansion
1 Space Race 3

8. Michigan 2 Hawaii 3 Massachusetts 1

9. Picasso 3 Michelangelo 1 Van Gogh 2

10. phonograph 1 telephone 3 light bulb 2

11. 6/7 3 2/3 1 4/5 2

12. Pearl Harbor 2 Kennedy Assassination 3
Great Depression 1

13. first space shuttle flight 3 first man on the
moon 1 Nixon resignation 2

14. Neil Armstrong 2 Sally Ride 3
John Glenn 1

15. Mark Twain 2 Ernest Hemingway 3
William Shakespeare 1

Page 183

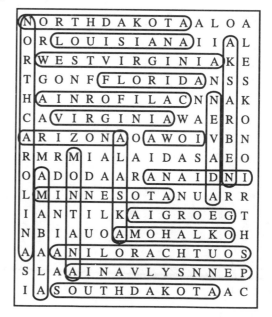

Page 185

You can if you think you can.

Answer Key (cont.)

1. F
2. O
3. N
4. H
5. A
6. U
7. Y
8. C
9. T
10. K
11. I

Page 186

1. Don't count your chickens before they hatch.
2. Birds of a feather flock together.
3. A stitch in time saves nine.
4. A penny saved is a penny earned.
5. Two wrongs don't make a right.
6. Where there is a will, there is a way.
7. Strike while the iron is hot.
8. A watched pot never boils.

Page 187

1. Look before you leap.
2. Never put off until tomorrow what can be done today.
3. A friend in need is a friend indeed.
4. The early bird catches the worm.
5. All that glitters is not gold.
6. Don't cry over spilled milk.
7. You never know what you can do til you try.
8. Make yourself necessary to someone.

Page 190

abecedarian—a person who is learning the

alphabet; a beginner

agglomerate—*v.* to gather into a rounded mass *n.* a mass of things clustered together.

agoraphobia—fear of open, public places

alopecia—loss of hair

aperture—an opening or an orifice

conundrum—a riddle or complicated problem

expurgate—to remove objectionable material from

hirsute—hairy

lacuna—a missing part of space; a gap

mellifluous—flowing smoothly and sweetly

obstreperous—noisy and unruly; defiant

piliferous—bearing or having hair

isthmus—a narrow strip of land connecting two larger land masses

sigillography—study of seals and signets

tessellate—to form or incorporate a mosaic pattern

ululate—to wail or howl loudly

ungulate—having hoofs

verboten—forbidden

Page 191

1. late date
2. fat rat
3. bad lad
4. rude dude
5. bug's mug (or bug mug)
6. long song
7. fat cat
8. double trouble
9. big pig
10. Swiss miss
11. bony pony
12. bright light
13. funny bunny

Answer Key (cont.)

14. glad lad

15. lazy daisy

16. sad dad

17. mouse house

18. no dough

19. cross boss

20. funny money

Page 192

1. ill Bill

2. bad lad

3. glum chum

4. shy fly

5. spunky monkey

6. plump ump

7. fluffy puppy

8. sad dad

9. wet pet

10. pink drink

11. steady Teddy

12. sloppy poppy

13. wee flea

14. sick chick

15. sharp harp

Page 193

1. noon

2. did

3. ewe

4. Bob

5. tot

6. peep

7. eye

8. pop or dad

9. dud

10. toot

11. bib

12. solos

13. mom or mum

14. kayak

15. level

16. pop

17. Answers will vary. They include Anna, Eve, Hannah, and Nan.

18. pup

19. deed

20. civic

Page 194

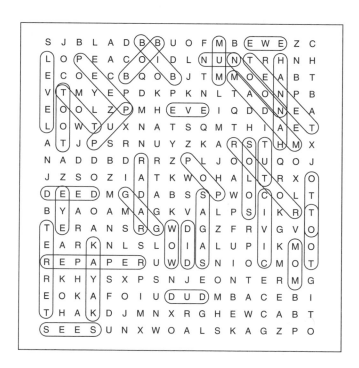

Page 195

Little Women - Louisa May Alcott

Anne of Green Gables - Lucy Maud Montgomery

A Wrinkle in Time - Madeline L'Engle

The Outsiders - S.E. Hinton

Answer Key (cont.)

Tom Sawyer - Mark Twain

Watership Down - Richard Adams

Bridge to Terabithia - Katherine Paterson

Jane Eyre - Charlotte Bronte

Little House on the Prairie - Laura Ingalls Wilder

Island of the Blue Dolphins - Scott O'Dell

Pages 201–206

1. Capital resources
2. Consumer
3. Economics
4. Demand
5. Goods
6. Services
7. Natural Resources
8. Profit
9. Cost
10. Producer
11. Supply
12. Wants
13. Needs
14. Opportunity Cost
15. Production
16. Human Resources
17. Rent
18. Wages or Salary
19. Scarcity
20. Entrepreneur
21. Employer
22. Employee
23. Specialization
24. Interest
25. Inflation
26. Recession
27. Stock
28. Investor
29. Competition
30. Division of Labor

Page 208

1. (35 divided by 5) x (27 divided by 3) = 63
2. (32 divided by 4) x (49 divided by 7) = 56
3. (72 divided by 9) x (24 divided by 8) = 24
4. (56 divided by 7) x (64 divided by 8) = 64
5. (36 divided by 6) x (35 divided by 7) = 30

Page 209

1. face to face
2. man overboard
3. split level
4. long underwear
5. deer crossing
6. head over heels
7. business before pleasure
8. order in the court
9. uptown
10. banana split
11. three degrees below zero
12. Minnesota

Page 210

1. scatterbrained
2. six feet below the ground
3. a square meal
4. neon light
5. little league
6. big man on campus
7. pain in the neck

Answer Key (cont.)

8. check up

9. Tiny Tim

10. once over lightly

11. keep it under your hat

12. high school

Page 212

81 / 9 x 6	9 x 9 / 3 x 6 / 7 x 8	4 x 5 / 2 x 10 / 2 x 6	63 / 6 x 7 / 64
54 / 7 x 4 / 3 x 7	56 / 28 / 5 x 12	3 x 4 / 16 / 3 x 5 / 4 x 8	4 x 16 / 15 / 9 x 6
21 / 33 / 9 x 5	6 x 10 / 3 x 11 / 7 / 44	32 / 49 x 7 / 42 / 12	4 x 9 / 6 x 7 / 36 ÷ 2
45 / 4 x 19	2 x 22 / 76 / 2 x 16	60 ÷ 5 / 8 x 4 / 5 x 5	3 x 6 / 50 ÷ 2

Page 214

It is better to have read some very interesting books than never to have read any at all.